CHRIST
ENLIGHTENED

THE LOST TEACHINGS OF JESUS UNVEILED

STEVEN S. SADLEIR

Christ Enlightened: The Lost Teachings of Jesus Unveiled

by Steven S. Sadleir

ISBN: 1-4392-6785-5

ISBN13: 9781439267851

Publisher:

Self Awareness Institute
668 North Coast Highway #417
Laguna Beach, CA 92651
www.SelfAwareness.com
949-355-3249

. . .

Bulk orders for colleges, libraries, and churches, or for speaking engagements, contact the Self Awareness Institute: info@SelfAwareness.com

©2010 Steven S. Sadleir

All rights reserved. No part of this publication may be reproduced, stored in a retrieval system, or transmitted, in any form or by any means—electronic, mechanical, photocopying, recording, or otherwise—without the prior written permission of the author.

Image on front cover is courtesy of www.PrintsofChrist.com

Prayer

Lord, guide me to say and do the right thing;
guide me in my research and writing
and the readers in their reading.
Guide us on our path to thee.
Enlighten us.

Preface

In 1974, during summer break from high school, I drove my Volkswagen Beetle up Interstate 395, along the east side of the Sierra Nevada Mountains of California. Turning into the solitude of the wilderness from a road stop called Independence, I climbed up to the highest peak of the Palisades Glacier to sit, meditate, and pray. It was there, looking down over the vast expanse of the Death Valley, that I received the inspiration to study and write about every religion, spiritual path, and philosophy on earth. Over the next twenty years I devoted myself to the research of over 250 groups, and met with many of the world's great spiritual teachers. In 1990 my first book, *Looking for God: A Seeker's Guide to Religious and Spiritual Groups of the World*, was published by Penguin and became an Amazon best seller. (It's now in its third edition.)

During my research on ancient Judaism and Christianity, I discovered a treasure trove of new information that was known to scholars but is still unfamiliar to most people—even Christians. So much that dates back to around the time of Christ has been dug up out of the desert in the last few decades that a much bigger, broader, and deeper understanding of early Christianity has emerged. The Lost Gospels of many of the other apostles have been discovered, translated, and recently published. Ancient Jewish Kabbalistic writings such as the

Zohar have only recently been translated into English and made available to the public; their contents reveal insights into Jewish mysticism that more clearly explain the meaning of what Jesus was teaching. Ancient books read by the Jewish Christians that we previously only had heard bits and pieces about from church fathers, the first popes, bishops and theologians, can now be read and studied. It's like taking a trip back to the first century. More information gives us greater clarity and insight into what Christ taught. What I discovered will amaze you. **This is the greatest story *never* told, within the greatest story *ever* told.**

As I began diving deeper into my biblical research, I was amazed how much information is out there that most people don't know exists or know very little about: the Dead Sea Scrolls, the Nag Hammadi Library, the Aramaic Bible or Peshitta, the Berlin Codex, the writings of the first church fathers, Josephus, the Kabbalah, and dozens of other sources that bring to light a much broader perspective of Christ's teachings during the first and second centuries than was previously known. Some of the most powerful teachings of Christ are virtually unknown to most Christians. Yet, these papyrus codexes were well known and read by the earliest Jewish Christians, those closest to Jesus himself. In these ancient gospels, his voice comes alive and his teaching becomes much clearer.

Early Christians gained a form of higher awareness through Jesus called *Gnosis*, from the Greek word meaning an enlightened awareness or experience. It wasn't just an understanding, as in knowledge of a philosophical idea or precept, but a place of expanded inner knowing—an awakened or higher state of consciousness. Having studied a great deal of Eastern philosophy and some Jewish mysticism, it became clear that the descriptions of the apostles' experiences of gnosis, for example the Pentecost, were similar to those described as *samadhi* by the Yogis of India and *nirvana* by the Buddhists. In the gnostic Christian literature, Jesus explains what *enlightenment* is and makes it clearer and easier to understand. In these ancient scriptures

Jesus reveals to us *the way* to enlightenment. He is bringing us to full God realization and gives us the key to the kingdom of heaven on earth.

All the recent archeological finds and research from the world's greatest scholars paints a whole new picture of those first hundred years before Christ, time during the life of Christ, and first hundred years after Christ, were like. Most of what we think of as Christ's teachings were given to us through the Greco-Roman culture three hundred years after Jesus lived, and much of what the earliest Jewish Christians believed was lost or intentionally hidden from public purview. For centuries lay people were not even allowed to own a Bible—for a Christian, owning a Bible was punishable by death. Even now many church authorities are leery about these new findings because they feel it threatens our faith. But my experience has been that these new perspectives add greater depth and meaning to Christ's teachings and make clearer the more obscure or confusing statements made in both the Old and New Testaments.

I invite you to look within, and pray for insight and guidance as you read this book. The findings and conclusions are startling and sometimes disconcerting, given what we have been taught, but this new information ultimately brought me closer to God and Christ, and I think it will bring you closer, too. Those things I questioned about church dogma or scriptural interpretation were more than made up for by the powerful love and insight that was received through Christ's word.

If you love Jesus, you owe it to yourself to learn all you can about what he said or what these earliest Christians believed he said. If you are not a Christian, I think you will find that the power and truth of these teachings will enlighten you. Just have faith.

Contents

1 The Fulfillment of Prophecy   1
The Age of Aquarius, the Age of Enlightenment, Nirvana, the Fulfillment of Biblical Prophecy, and the Current Reformation.

2 Abraham and the Ancient World   15
The Sumerians, the Epic of Gilgamesh, the Harappn Culture, Egyptian Civilization, Zoroastrianism, Ur, the Migration of Abraham, the Canaanite god El, Abraham's Journey, Patriarchs and Prophets, and Moses.

3 Judaism and the Messiah   39
The Essenes, the Dead Sea Scrolls, Jewish Apocrypha and Pseudepigrapha, the Merkabah, the Axial Age, the Kabbalah, Our Fall from Grace, and the Messiah.

4 Jeshua ben Joseph the Christ   65
The Aramaic Gospels, Jewish Christians, Jesus Teaches the way, the Gospel of the Ebionites, the Gospel of the Nazareans, the Gospel of the Hebrews, the Gospel of the Egyptians, the Dialog with the Savior, and the Thunder Perfect Mind.

5	**The Apostles' Canon**	89

The Twelve Apostles, New Testament Apostles, the Apostle Thomas, The Gospel of Thomas, the Book of Thomas the Contender, the Saint Thomas Christians from India, the Apostle James, the Gospel of James, the Apostle Philip and the Gospel of Philip, Mary Magdalene, the Gospel of Mary Magdalene and the Magdalene Papyrus.

6	**Gnosticism**	125

The Apostle Peter, the Apocalypse of Peter, Gnostic Proliferation, Sethian Gnosticism, the Secret Book of John, the Gospel of Judas Iscariot, the Infancy Gospels, Valentnianism, and the Gospel of Truth.

7	**Saint Paul's Christianity**	151

Paul's Greco-Roman World; the New Testament; the Apostolic Fathers; Sin, Hell, and Redemption; the Church Fathers; Emperor Constantine; the Council of Nicaea; and the Conclusion.

About the Author — 195

References — 196

Acknowledgements

This book is a synthesis of the work of many scholars, done over many years, and they all should be acknowledged, especially those whose works are quoted or listed as references in this book. I highly recommend that every sincere student of Christ read these works and come to their own conclusions.

A special thanks to Justine Amodeo for her keen insight, good ideas, and editing, and also to the entire publishing team at CreateSpace/Amazon. Thank you to Jim Smith and David Smith for their candid feedback and encouragement, John Furino for his insights, and to Mia Worley for her hard work and support. I would also like to thank the faculty and students of the Self Awareness Institute for their candid feedback and encouragement, and all the spiritual masters, teachers, and clergy who have helped guide me along the way.

I would also like to thank my late Grandma Ruth for all those Bible studies, and for introducing me to Jesus. I thank Dr. Robert Schuller and the Reverend Minasian for inspiring me to learn more about Christ. From the depths of my soul, I thank Christ for his presence in my life, and God to whom I bow and offer this book in devotion. Thank you, God, thank you, a thousand times, thank you.

Introduction

In order to provide a complete and clear picture of what Jesus was teaching, we need to create a clearer context in which his coming was received, and what the prophesy was, or is, to his people. So I begin by explaining the world's global perspectives of prophesy and it's fulfillment, and bring to light the radical spiritual movement that is occurring in the world today. However, to really understand Christianity, you need to go back to the very beginning of recorded history and see how the biblical God was created and developed over time. This leads us to Abraham, the patriarch of Judaism, Christianity, and Islam. We are going to look at who the Hebrews were, and what the Jews believed throughout their long history. For it was Abraham's revelation that led to our current understanding of God and the belief in a fulfillment of prophesy. So we are going to take a good look at the Sumerian culture in which Abraham was born, and gain a clearer picture of the backgrounds of the Hebrew and Semite cultures of his day. We will also look at how other ancient civilizations influenced the Bible, including the Canaanite, Egyptian, Persian and Harrappan cultures.

We will then explore the events that led to the expectation of a messiah and document the history of this age, including: Roman history, Philo of Alexandria, the Annals of Rome, and Josephus. We will review the Dead Sea Scrolls of Qumran, the Pseudepigrapha and Apocrypha, rabbinical writings before the destruction of the temple, the Targums and Aramaic texts, and the Jewish Magical Papyri. We will also look at the Essenes and Jewish esoteric teachings of the Kabbalah, including the Sefirot, the Bahir, and the Zohar. We are also going to look at the Egyptian Book of the Dead, the Epic of Gilgamesh, Zoroastrianism, as well as Greek and Hermetic writings and the Mithran cults. By studying these writings we gain a much better understanding of what the world was like during Christ's time, and thereby gain a better understanding of who the messiah is and what role he plays.

The focus of this book will be on the lost teachings of Jesus and the Gnostic gospels, as revealed through the Nag Hammadi library, the Berlin Codex, the Aramaic Peshitta, and other recently found codex's (papyrus books) dating back to the first and second centuries, as well as the earliest epistles of the apostolic fathers, church fathers and the apologists. We will place great emphasis on what both the Old and New Testaments say, and gain insights from the Jewish Talmud. The focus of our study is on the earliest Jewish Christian Gospels that are still unknown to most people, including the gospels of Thomas, James, Philip, and Mary, as well as those of the Hebrews, Egyptians, Nazarenes, and Ebonite's. Over eleven volumes of Christ's word dating from the first and second centuries are unveiled and explained.

We will also delve deeply into the Gnostic philosophy and compare it to the Pali Canon of the Buddha, the Vedas, and Upanishads of India, and other Eastern and esoteric teachings. We will also explore the history of the early church, from St. Paul to the Council of Nicea, and the many reinventions of Christianity to modern times. When you are finished with this book, you will have a greater understanding of the history and context of Christ's teachings than most clergy, and in so doing, you will gain greater understanding and faith.

My intention is to provide the information as objectively as I can so you may form your own opinions and draw your own conclusions. I offer my interpretations of these cryptic texts, based on years of discussions with the world's leading experts and my own personal experience. I believe that your spirit will guide you as you are reading and that you will come to know the truth for yourself if you keep an open mind and open heart; just reflect and pray. What has been revealed is amazing; it's rewriting Christian history and theology. We live in an exciting time in the history of the world as this information is coming to light, and you are amongst the first to realize it for yourself. You are among the first to be *Christ Enlightened*.

The Fulfillment of Prophesy

It happened at a time when man had learned to fly. As he took to the heavens to explore his outer universe, he also began to look within and discover his own inner nature. At the same time we learned about the physical universe and biology, we developed greater awareness of how our mind works and of the subtle nature of our consciousness. Within this generation we have witnessed man walking on the moon, a technological revolution that has brought the world together, and an awakening of human consciousness never seen before in the history of mankind. Millions of people are reading about raising their consciousness; it's on the Internet, television, the radio, and in the movies. And just as meditation is going mainstream, the Egyptian desert gives up Christ's teachings on enlightenment that were buried beneath the sand for over two thousand years. It is no coincidence. We live in a prophetic age; we live in the age of enlightenment.

Throughout history, throughout the world, tribes and civilizations have passed on stories of man having lived in a *golden age*, a paradise on earth, at some time in antiquity, before falling into a cycle of darkness and living in ignorance of our divine nature, and eventually returning to the light during an age of enlightenment, or a heaven on earth, once again. This paradigm is deeply engrained in our collective consciousness; it's a global mythology.

What is an *age*? In Giorgio de Santillana's book *Hamlet's Mill*, he cites over 200 mythologies that refer to the movement of the stars and of ages, and historian Joseph Campbell in *The Hero with a Thousand Faces* cites the recurring theme of a coming new age and humans living in a heaven on earth. Christians have been expecting a new age for over two thousand years. What makes this universal mythology so incredible is that the consensus is that we are now living in that age. This is the dawning of the age of Aquarius.

The Age of Aquarius

Ancient man looked up at the stars and traced lines between them and saw images (constellations) emerge. Those who inhabited the Hellenized (Greek) world called these images or signs: Aries the ram, Taurus the bull, Gemini the twins, Cancer the crab, Leo the lion, Virgo the virgin, Libra the scales, Scorpio the scorpion, Sagittarius the centaur, Capricorn the goat, Aquarius the water bearer, and Pisces the fish. In this system, each constellation is represented by one of the twelve signs of the zodiac. Each sign represents a different series of conditions that we souls go through; like the seasons of the year, the great cosmic time clock in the sky represents a cosmic cycle of life, death, and renewal.

As the earth rotates around the sun it passes through each sign of the zodiac like the hands of a clock sweeping around on a solar orbit that repeats each solar year. However, astrological ages proceed in the opposite direction from our annual rotation; so rather than going from the sign of Aquarius to Pisces as our solar rotation goes (January to February to March), the earth's rotational *axis* (the line that runs through the poles) is slowly going the other way, from Pisces to Aquarius. Over 25,771.5 years the earth wobbles on its axis (like a top spinning) and points to different constellations through what is called the precession of the equinoxes. The earth spends approximately 2,150 years in each sign of the zodiac. Each sign represents a different set of opportunities and challenges, as do the seasons of the solar year.

The Piscean age was represented by the fish, one of the original symbols for Jesus and the way, about 2,150 years ago. This is a water sign, and this age was marked by oceanic travel and exploration of the water and discovery made by crossing over water. It is represented by medicine, chemicals, and exploration, and is expressed through belief and faith. In contrast, the age of Aquarius is marked by energy and information through the air. Technological developments such as satellites, cell phones, and the Internet are all indicative of Aquarius. Space travel and meditation are very Aquarian. Aquarius is the water bearer—**a man bearing a pitcher of water**—and he is the *humanitarian* heralding the age of Enlightenment and peace on earth.

This Aquarian age is the age in which man's spiritual nature will awaken, and the world will live in peace as God intended. During this age man realizes God's presence within himself and on the earth. It's in the Old Testament, it's in the Kabbalah, and it's in the New Testament. Jesus tells us of this second coming in *Luke* (22:10):

> *"When will you come again? And Jesus replies* ***'A man will meet you bearing a pitcher of water.'"***

So, did Jesus mean that a physical man with a pitcher of water would come up to one or all of the disciples while they were still living or was he referring to the current age of Aquarius? The symbol of a man bearing a pitcher of water representing Aquarius was familiar to people living in the Middle East in the first century. None of the gospels tell us of any apostles meeting a man bearing a pitcher, but everyone in Western civilization has heard of Aquarius and the symbol of the water bearer is familiar to us, perhaps more now than in Christ's day.

As we enter this age of Aquarius, we are all being greeted by the *man bearing a pitcher of water.*

The Age of Enlightenment

In the East, epochs are called *yugas*. The four yugas are: the Satya yuga (or Krita yuga), the Treta yuga, the Dvapara yuga, and the Kali yuga or age of darkness; these also complete an approximately 26,000 year cycle. We've been living in the Kali yuga. According to the Sanatana Dharma revealed by the Rishi's of India and recorded in the Vedas, mankind has fallen asleep and become unconscious of our own intrinsic nature as spirit; we've become dulled through our mind and senses and lost our way. We suffer because we have forgotten who we are, and we have lost touch with the divine presence on earth. The good news is that we are entering this age of enlightenment; we are entering the Satya yuga—the age where human beings will remember who they are and why they were born. In this age, people will begin to create the world that we intrinsically want to live in. We will enlighten our consciousness collectively and live in peace on earth. In the Satya yuga we live with God in heaven on earth.

A yogi might say that we become one in Christ consciousness, as they all recognize that Christ was enlightened; he is what they would call an *avatar* or incarnation of the divine in human form. When Jesus said in John 10:31 "I and my Father are one" (or "my father and I are one"), he was expressing a universal truth; we are one in spirit. We are all one in spirit. There is a state of consciousness in which you will join him in consciousness, even while the flesh breathes. God dwells everywhere, so when you realize the divine presence within you, you also realize that same divine presence in everyone else and in everything else, everywhere, all the time. This is God realization.

The declaration in Luke 17:21 "The Kingdom of God is within you" (more liberally quoted as "the Kingdom of Heaven lies within") refers to the state of enlightenment, in which we realize the full effulgence of God's grace as an indescribable bliss that is now being experienced all over the world. The yogi's call this blissful state Samadhi. Finding the "Kingdom of God within you" is one of the most universal esoteric teachings and the basis of most paths to enlightenment. Christianity is, after all, an Eastern teaching, and Christ's words echo the wisdom of the Eastern tradition.

During the twenty years of research for my book on world religions, *Looking for God: A Seeker's Guide to Religious and Spiritual Groups of the World*, I had occasion to sit and learn from dozens of enlightened masters from all over the world. All of them recognized this current age as the beginning of the age of enlightenment. One of the first Eastern masters to be known through the mass media in the West was **Maharishi Mahesh Yogi**, the founder of *TM* or Transcendental Meditation. In Maharishi's book *The Age of Enlightenment* he announces the beginning of an age where the collective consciousness of humanity would awaken and become enlightened. His movement helped grow this awareness throughout Western civilization, and through his affiliation with the rock group the Beatles many new concepts of higher awareness such as instant karma were introduced to the occidental world. Beginning in the 1960s and through the 1970s, music served as a harbinger of the coming age, with songs like "The Age of Aquarius" from the play *Hair* and the Beatles hit "Within you, Without You," planting the seeds of consciousness that are now sprouting.

Vethathiri Maharishi, the master with whom I apprenticed for many years, taught that our latent faculties of higher awareness were still developing up on the crown of our head (frontal and temporal lobes of the neo-cortex). By learning to direct our mind we can activate our sixth sense and remember who we are and why we were born. As the student directs his or her attention to the point between the eyebrows known as the third eye, his or her life force energy or spirit rises to the uppermost regions of the brain, causing a radical awakening of consciousness. Experiences similar to the Pentecost may also occur, like seeing tongues of fames, the sound of a mighty wind, and utterances. Like working out a muscle, as you meditate, you develop these neurological pathways that get bigger and stronger, and inner clarity develops. Meditation awakens consciousness. In 1990, I sat in meditation for twenty-three hours a day for forty consecutive days and nights under the guidance of the arch yogi **Sri Sri Sri Shivabalayogi Maharaj** in Bangalore; for it is when the mind turns inward to the source, the true nature of the self is realized—God is realized. Everyone can have God realization. This awakening of consciousness is being experienced by thousands of people around the world even now—the consciousness of humanity is awakening en masse.

The Satya yuga is the age of truth, in which we awaken from the dream of unknowing and the reality of God's living presence is realized within us and around us everywhere, all the time; it is the age when we live as spirit and walk with God in heaven on earth. This is a time when people become enlightened. This is a time when the highest potential is realized within human beings. It's Eden. This era will be recognized when millions of people begin meditating again; it's a sign. In the Hindu epic the Mahabharata, the last age of enlightenment or Krita yuga is described as a place and time when all people are happy and live in peace:

> [T]here were no poor and no rich; there was no need to labor, because all that men required was obtained by the power of will; the chief virtue was the abandonment of all worldly desires. The Krita Yuga was without disease; there was no lessening with the years; there was no hatred or vanity, or evil thought; no sorrow, no fear. All mankind could attain to supreme blessedness...

Nirvana

Five hundred years before Christ was born, a young prince named Siddhartha Gautama lived in a kingdom that is now a part of Nepal and northern India . As a prince, Siddhartha had been sheltered from much of the pain and suffering of this world, and when he discovered it as a young man, it moved him so much that he left his palace and family to become a yogi. Siddhartha meditated for many years and ultimately became enlightened and was known as the Buddha or the enlightened one.

Buddha's method for attaining enlightenment was very simple and direct—meditate. Later all kinds of philosophical systems were developed under the name of Buddhism, but the path to enlightenment centers on meditation. Buddha's Shakti (spiritual energy) was so strong from his years of meditation that others would become enlightened by just being in his presence. Like Jesus, within a few hundred years Buddha went from being an enlightened master to becoming a god in the eyes of his devotees, and his teaching went from meditation and looking within to a complex system of rituals and rules of conduct and a hierarchical priesthood, similar to Catholicism. The Bodhisattva, or Buddhist practitioner, dedicates their effort to the enlightenment of the world. The belief is that when the whole of humanity becomes enlightened we will create a heaven on earth—Nirvana.

In the Dhammapada the Buddha states that nirvana is "the highest happiness." This happiness is not the kind derived from impermanent things, but of an enduring and transcendental nature that is beyond conception and only attained through *Bodhi* – enlightenment. Nirvana is a state of consciousness that is unconditioned (*asankhata*), as the consciousness is unfettered with the passions of the mind and senses it is freed from them, that is, the consciousness is liberated. The goal of practicing Buddhism is to awaken from the "sleep of ignorance" through the realization of our true nature—gnosis or nirvana. Understanding these Eastern concepts that preceded Christ will help us understand the cryptic messages of Christ.

Separated by five hundred years and over three thousand miles, the lives, deeds, and teaching of the Buddha and of Christ are remarkably similar. But this should not surprise us if those teaching are truly universal. In Marcus Borg and Jack Kornfield's book *Jesus and Buddha: The Parallel Saying*, they cite dozens of examples of these striking similarities, such as:

> Jesus: "Do unto others as you would have them do unto you."
> Buddha: "Consider others as yourself."
>
> Jesus: "Give unto anyone who requests it."
> Buddha: "Give when you are asked."

During the past few decades, Buddhist philosophy has gone mainstream in the West, and Buddhist practice is growing into millions. His holiness the **Dalai Lama** of Tibet, a leading figure in Buddhism and a Nobel Peace Prize winner, is known around the world, and his message of compassion, tolerance, and peace have inspired millions. We live in an age where millions of people are now meditating and practicing mindfulness, much like the early Christians. The enlightened Buddhist masters realize that we live in an age of enlightenment. We are all coming together regardless of our nationality, race, religion, or gender to create a better world. We have entered the age of enlightenment, we are entering Eden, and we are realizing nirvana.

In the East we see that a golden age is dawning; through the arcane teachings and mystery schools we learn that this age is a time of global awakening, and it's part of the native and indigenous traditions too. While conducting research for my book *Looking for God: A Seeker's Guide to Religious and Spiritual Groups of the World*, I traveled to places like the backwoods of Borneo, the Australian outback, and the Himalayas to speak with elders of ancient cultures to learn their wisdom before their cultures were destroyed. They all recognized the dawning of a golden age of higher awareness. I spent years meeting with shamans from Incan, Mayan and numerous Native American traditions, and all of them hold the belief that this current era is an auspicious time when the consciousness of humanity awakens. I have studied with Zen masters, Tibetan masters, Taoist Masters, Siddha masters, Sufi Masters, Kundalini masters, Shaktipat masters, and many others, and they all recognize the awakening of consciousness that is occurring on the planet right now. This belief shows up all over the world, but nowhere is it as clearly stated as in the Bible.

The Fulfillment of Biblical Prophesy

According to Jewish biblical prophecy God promised Abraham the land now called Israel as a place where Abraham's descendants, the Jews, could propagate and prosper. The point was not who the Messiah was or what miracles he might perform, but that the result would be that Jews had their sacred land and self-determination—their own state of Israel. During the over 4,000 years of Jewish history, Jews have only had their kingdom during parts of the reign of Kings David and Solomon, and brief reigns before and after Phoenician, Philistine, Assyrian, and Babylonian conquest and captivity. Clearly, God had not fulfilled his promise yet, but after World War II that changed. The Holocaust in Nazi Europe killed around six million Jews, but it uprooted even more, and after the war, Jews began migrating to Israel in a mass Zionist movement, creating a power struggle with the Palestinian people who lived there. After years of fighting, Israel gained statehood in 1949, and for the first time in history, the Jews had their homeland—as promised—the prophesy is being fulfilled.

Israel's presence in the Middle East is somewhat of a miracle in itself because it is surrounded by nations that have sworn to remove it from the face of the earth and yet it thrives. Historically, Babylon has been the nemesis of the Jewish people, and in this generation we have already fought two World Wars against Babylon—modern Baghdad, Iraq; it's biblical. The Jews now have their homeland, and they are propagating. The Jewish prophecy is being fulfilled. Moreover, as Christ is the word and we can witness how his word has arisen again in these ancient papyrus books that have been buried in the desert sands of Egypt for thousands of years. Only now are they surfacing, at a time when the world is, at last, ready to receive it. There is literally **a second coming of Christ's word**. The spirit is with his word and his word is coming to us now that we are ready to receive him and understand the deeper meaning of his teachings. Now we are beginning to understand what enlightenment means, so now we can understand what Jesus was teaching. Moreover, according to Rabbi Philip S. Berg, head of the Research Center for Kabbalah, the Bible tells us we have now entered this **messianic age**. According to these messianic Jews the age of the Messiah is upon us.

We have only to observe what has occurred during this current generation to see that the world is becoming enlightened before our very eyes. Look at the signs: just a few decades ago black people had to sit in the back of the bus and were denied many privileges and rights as citizens, and now the United States has a black president—**Barak Obama**. Our consciousness shifted significantly over the last few decades and that is invoking a social change. As we evolved in consciousness women, minorities, and people with disabilities all began to gain more rights and public support. We, as a society, are showing more compassion, we are evolving in consciousness.

Consciousness is a growing subject showing up in movies, radio, and television shows; consciousness is being discussed on the most-watched television program –of all time—**Oprah**. Some of our best-selling authors like Deepak Chopra, Wayne Dyer, and Eckhart Tolle are teaching how to become more conscious. The signs are everywhere. Many of the books cited in this work are best sellers, and I recommend that you read them. The History Channel, A&E, and National Geographic television networks have programming that addresses the Gnostic gospels and the hidden teachings of Jesus; watch them and form your own conclusions. We live during a spiritual renaissance. The information that I have been sharing with you rests on the shoulders of hundreds of scholars who are bringing to life what actually happened in the first few centuries of Christian history. Now, it's in front of our face, and we can't ignore it any longer.

In terms of one's individual life this shift appears to occur very slowly because we can so clearly see what still needs to change, but over the course of human existence the shift that has already occurred in the last fifty years is unprecedented. The first signs of this major shift began during the **American Revolution**, around 200 years ago—a time often called the age of enlightenment. In 1776 a small group of idealists known to us as the founding fathers put forth a vision of a better world and the spirit behind those ideas had such a force that it was able to conquer the greatest force known in its day—the British Empire. From this vision, the whole world has changed; democracy and the right to life, liberty, and the pursuit of happiness are now an international standard for civilization. We would not have guessed the Berlin Wall would come down or that the Soviet Union would collapse, just years before they did; the change is happening fast, and it's accelerating. The Internet, phone, and media have brought the world together, and now people all over the world—Jews, Christians, Muslims, Buddhists, Hindus, and atheists—are all sharing information and learning about each other's beliefs. This cross fertilization of spiritual ideas is fostering a global awakening of consciousness.

The Current Reformation

We are currently experiencing a modern reformation. The first Reformation occurred during the fourteenth and fifteenth centuries. Before this time, the Catholic Church had complete authority over all theology and information about Jesus and Christianity; the church had complete power over not only the word of God but also the politics and finances of the Holy Roman Empire. The church was not to be questioned—you could be put to death for that. The church gained power through fear. Representatives of the pope sat in every court in Europe. The church was the center of money and power, and, consequently, abuses of the church were growing stronger creating disillusionment and discontent amongst the clergy throughout the continent.

The printing press had just been invented, and the book that was in most demand was the Bible. However, in most countries mere ownership of a Bible by a layman was punishable by death. The church made it very clear that for their own good, Christians should not try to interpret the Bible for themselves. The first of a series of disruptive new perspectives came from **John Wycliffe** at Oxford University in England, and then **Jan Huss** at the University of Prague, (in the modern Czech Republic). These radicals were telling the public what the Bible actually says and wanted to use it as the authoritative source of God's word, but this countermanded the authority of the church in Rome. So, after the Council of Constance (1414-1417) the bishops condemned Jan Huss and burned him alive at the stake. They couldn't bring Wycliffe to justice, so they posthumously burned him as a heretic for bringing an English Bible to the English-speaking people. The church hated him so much that many years after his death, they dug up his bones out of the grave and burned them.

The Reformation itself is generally believed to have begun on October 31, 1517, in Wittenberg, Saxony (Germany), after a German cleric named **Marten Luther** nailed his *Ninety-Five Theses* to the door of the All Saint's Church, which served as a notice board for university-related announcements. Luther was protesting, and challenging the pope for preaching what the clergy considered "false doctrines," malpractice, the "sale of indulgences," and keeping the word of God from the people. This *protest movement* or Protestantism spread further into Switzerland through reformers like **Ulrich Zwingli** and Frenchmen **John Calvin** who had followings in Scotland, Hungary, Germany, Switzerland, and elsewhere. Geneva became the unofficial capital of the Protestant movement. The Church of England (Anglican Church) was formed when **King Henry VIII** famously tried in vain to get his marriage to Catherine annulled so he could re-marry and increase his chances of obtaining a male heir. The pope rejected the annulment, so Henry aligned with the Protestants and converted the whole country to Protestantism with an edict. These reformers had all questioned the authority of the church to dictate the word of God, and they used their own minds to determine the truth for themselves through independent investigation, reflection and prayer.

As new information about the word of God became publicly available, the people began to think for themselves too. Their view of Christianity and what Christ taught changed as they began independent investigations into what had been written. They found that what was written and its meaning were different from what they had been told to believe and not to question. But the truth brought a lot more people closer to Christ and continues to. The church was fearful of not having power over the people and of Christians determining for themselves the meaning of Christ's word. The church preached that laymen couldn't understand the true meaning in the Bible and threatened that to listen to any other source for information about God or Christ would be cause for going to Hell. It tried to keep people from thinking for themselves by putting the fear of God in them—they were told to "be like sheep" and not question the dogma, interpretations, or authority of the church. As a direct result, religion has been the primary cause, or excuse, for war and persecution throughout the world throughout history.

We are now in a similar situation, laymen are being given access to information about Jesus, early Christianity, and Christ's teaching that contradicts, to some extent, what our churches have been telling us. Much of this information has been kept secret, destroyed, lost, or deliberately ignored so we would not discover it. Moreover, this new information about Christ is being rejected, denied, and marginalized by those who haven't even studied it yet. Many churches are threatened by these new findings and are steering congregants away from doing independent research, as if there was something there you shouldn't see or know or you would not able to discern the truth for yourself. But despite these attempts to discount these historical facts, more information keeps entering the public domain. The world as we know it is changing, Christianity is changing, and it is good. Despite a disinformation movement that is trying to keep people from knowing the truth, the truth is entering the collective consciousness of the planet. The fact that you are reading this book is proof.

Those who don't think for themselves or who simply ignore or discount other ideological positions are, by definition, ignorant; those who just blindly follow another or believe whatever they are told are in a cult. If you are told not to question what you are told, you are in a cult. If you are told not to think for yourself, you are being deceived, and Jesus warns us about this. Jesus came from a tradition of questioning God's word in order to better understand it, and this is what Jesus taught.

At one point in history the church killed people with contrary views. But we can no longer deny that the earth rotates around the sun and not the other way around. At one time these new ideas threatened the church, but how does science and a new scientific discovery keep us from God? We learn more about God and his creation through science than by any other means. There are Christians today who still deny evolution and believe that the devil somehow buried dinosaur bones to trick us and test our faith. Jews recognize their story of creation in Genesis as a metaphor; evolution is the proof of God's living and guiding presence with us and within us. There are those who just stubbornly refuse to even look at all the new information coming to light in this century, and some evangelical churches are grossly misrepresenting these Gnostic teachings in a clear effort to dissuade congregants from learning for themselves. Most people are still living in ignorance. However, the depth of his teachings are now coming to light nonetheless, and they are powerful. To deny these new insights is to deny the word of God. So let's look at all the facts, and then you can decide for yourself.

. . .

Abraham and the Ancient World

Who invented God? The oldest artifact depicting what is believed to be a deity is what appears to be a fertility goddess carved from mammoth ivory, dating back some 35,000 years discovered in Germany. So was our first god a woman? Early man recognized both the male and female aspects of the Divine. The idea of God is reflected in some of the earliest records of human history. God was typically related to the heavens, the Creator, the giver of life, and, generally, compassionate and loving to those he created. He is most often considered the One from which all things arise, by whom we are sustained and guided, and to whom we ultimately return. Throughout history, these attributes are given different names in various cultures, but this paradigm of God is universal. Here we are going to explore the primary cultures—Sumerian, Harrappan, Egyptian, Persian and Hebrew—that were developing some of the first ideas of God ever recorded - and observe how these ideas developed into the concept of monotheism as taught through the Bible today.

Jesus Christ's relevance in our life is founded in the belief and fulfillment of an ancient Jewish prophesy telling of an messianic period in which the Jewish people would be freed from foreign oppression, and be fruitful and multiply in Canaan, the land God promised Abraham, roughly modern Palestine and Israel (Genesis 12). To help us understand the context of this prophesy, and it's fulfillment, we are going to look at the world as it was during the time of the patriarch Abraham and follow the history and theological development of God leading up to Abraham, then to Christ, and to this moment.

As we begin speaking about Judaism, it is important to understand that we are talking about a religion, a culture, *and* a race or races of people; we are referring broadly to the Semitic peoples of the Middle East. Shemites (Semites) are the decedents Shem, the son of Noah (who built the great Ark during the Great Biblical Flood) and include the Akkadians, Canaanites, Phoenicians, Arabs, and Ethiopians but more specifically typically refer to one Semitic group called the **Hebrews**, and later called the **Israelites**. Accounts of Abraham's life and teachings vary considerably between Judaism, Christianity, and Islam, as well as with the historical record. Abraham is featured in the book of Genesis and is regarded as the patriarch of Jewish, Christian, and Muslim traditions and of the Israelites, Ishmaelites, and Edomite peoples.

From the Bible we learn that Abraham's father was Terah, and his grandfather was Nahor, who lived in the cradle of civilization known as the Fertile Crescent or Mesopotamia (the land between two rivers), roughly modern Iraq. According to Jewish tradition, Abraham lived around 2123-1948 BCE (before the common era). Christian tradition and historical evidence places him 2000 to 1825 BCE, so when speaking of Abraham we are going back approximately 4,000 years—2,000 years before Christ. According to the book of Genesis, Abraham was led by God from Mesopotamia to the land of Canaan. There Abraham entered into a covenant with God: in exchange for sole recognition of God as the supreme universal deity and authority, God promises Abraham (Genesis 22:17):

> **That in blessing I will bless thee, and in multiplying I will multiply thy seed as the stars in heaven, and as the sand which is upon the sea shore.**

We are told in the Bible that Abraham was born in Ur, in Mesopotamia. The Jewish/Roman historian Josephus and Jewish authorities like the Maimonides believed that Ur of the Chaldees was in northern Mesopotamia, which is now a part of southeastern Turkey, identified with the city of Urartu. Whereas most scholars identify Ur as Urfa, which is located southeast of Baghdad, Iraq, along the Euphrates River, in one of the most oil-rich areas of the world. Both locations were influenced by the Sumerian culture that spread throughout Mesopotamia and was the dominant culture of that region in Abraham's time. Abraham was born in a land called Sumer within a culture called Sumerian. To fully grasp the evolution of our understanding of God, we must go back thousands of years to Sumerian civilization, arguably the oldest in recorded history.

The Sumerians

The term Sumerian refers to those speaking the Sumerian language, and the people of Sumer who lived along the Euphrates-Tigris alluvial plain in Mesopotamia, in what is recognized as Iraq today. Known as the cradle of civilization, the first settlements date back to Eridu in the Ubaid period late sixth millennium BCE. Abraham is believed to have lived during the Ur III period circa 2047-1940 BCE, sometimes referred to as the Sumerian Renaissance. During this period, there was a rise in the migration of Semitic people, some probably slaves, followed by waves of Martu or Amorites who later founded the Babylonian Empire.

The Sumerian people who settled here in the early Ubaid period (5300-4700 BCE) farmed the lands, which were made fertile by silt deposited by the Tigris and Euphrates Rivers. They were among the first to use irrigation, which enabled them to farm year round and stay in one place, as opposed to being hunters and gatherers who roamed constantly in search of food. Sumerians were amongst the first to create a written language; examples of Sumerian pre-cuneiform script on tablets that date to around 3500 BCE have been discovered. Their civilization was organized with city-states, and they were amongst the first to organize armies that included chariots drawn by horses and to build boats.

Many scholars today credit the Sumerians with inventing the wheel, initially from a potter's wheel, and later for vehicles and mills. Sumerians were also among the first astrologers, mapping the the constellations, many of which were recognized by the ancient Greeks and remain in the Zodiac that survives today. The five planets that are visible with the naked eye from earth all have Sumerian names. They also invented and developed arithmetic, using both a base-ten and a base-six numbering system. They developed the first known codified legal and administrative systems, messaging, schools, written history, and mail. They also traded with the other emerging civilizations extending as far as modern Afghanistan, Bahrain, Lebanon, and the Indus Valley civilization and Harrappan Culture of India.

Sumer was a polytheistic society, and its people served the gods that were represented in the form of man-made statues. The Sumerians are believed to be the first people to record their beliefs; this was thousands of years before any biblical records that survive today or even that are known to have exited. Each city-state had its own patrons, temples, and priest-kings. The Sumerians had a high god of the heavens named **An** (later **Anu**) who was the sky god, the god of heaven, lord of the constellations, the king of gods, and creator of the universe. His appearance is recognized by a royal tiara represented by two pair of bull horns. He had several consorts, including Ki (earth), Nammu, and Uras. Sumerians believed that God had created humans out of clay in order to serve him.

An, the oldest of the gods in the Sumerian pantheon, formed a triad with Enlil (later Marduk), and Enki. He was called Anu by the Akkadians, the rulers of Mesopotamia after the conquest of Sumer in 2334 BCE by King Sargon of Akkad. Anu came to be regarded as the father and first among gods; he is referred to in the famous *Epic of Gilgamesh*, the first piece of literature in history. The son of Lugalbanda, Gilgamesh is believed to be the fifth king of Uruk in the early dynastic II era ruling 2700 BCE, according to the Sumerian King List. Thus he lived approximately 700 years before Abraham, around the time of Noah (Genesis 5-6).

The Epic of Gilgamesh

The *Epic of Gilgamesh* is preserved on twelve clay tablets in the library collection of the seventh century BCE Assyrian king Ashurbanipal. The earliest Sumerian version dates to the Third Dynasty of Ur (2150-2000 BCE), which was during Abraham's time, so he would have known this story. The *Epic of Gilgamesh* dates back approximately to the time of the great flood recorded in the Bible, and the great flood is also recorded in the *Epic of Gilgamesh*, which supports the assertion that there was a great flood during this period. However, this flood only covered the the world that they knew, that is, the Sumerian civilization. Ur lies in the alluvial plain where four great rivers used to flow but now only two remain—the Tigris and Euphrates. The climate was wetter then, and the land was subject to flooding; during one of these floods, the great flood, most of the civilization of Sumer was destroyed - but not the whole world.

In the *Epic of Gilgamesh* we are told about Gilgamesh who was "the greatest king who ever lived, two-thirds god and one-third man." He was the strongest king-god who ever existed and built the great brick walls of Uruk that protected the people from invasions and flooding. *The Epic of Gilgamesh* is the story of "how a man becomes civilized, how he learns to rule himself and therefore his people, and to act with temperance, wisdom and piety," according to Stephen Mitchel in his English translation of the epic. Within the story is a description of how a large ship (an ark) weathers this great flood, the release and return of a dove, and the final resting of this ark on the mountains of Nizir, similar to Noah's account in Genesis (8:9).

We are told that man is formed from the dust of the ground and becomes a living being, the original man himself—natural, innocent, and solitary. An, the fatherly supreme god from heaven, guides and tests Gilgamesh to develop him into a great servant of god. There is also an underworld and a seeking of purpose and salvation; Gilgamesh is seeking eternal life. The epic's theme involves one transcendent god, who judges humanity and creates a great flood to purify the world, a savior who comes to redeem humanity and the quest for eternal life with god, all from the land where Abraham was born. Thus the Sumerians and Hebrews share both a common history and theology, and we have an independent validation that a great flood did occur during this biblical period. We also see from these accounts how these stories become embellished over time, which is why we don't want to interpret these mythologies too literally.

The opening passage of book one in Stephen Mitchel's *Epic of Gilgamesh* reads:

> Surpassing all kings, powerful and tall beyond all others, violent, splendid, a wild bull of a man, unvanquished leader, hero in the front lines, beloved by his soldiers -*fortress* they call him, *protector of the people, and the raging flood that destroys all defenses*- two thirds divine and one-third human, son of King Lugalbanda, who became god, and of the goddess Ninsun, he opened the mountain passes, dug wells on the slopes, crossed the vast ocean, sailed to the rising sun, journeyed to the edge of the world, in search of eternal life, and once he found Utnapishtim – the man who survived the Great Flood and was made immortal –he brought back the ancient, forgotten rites, restoring the temples that the Flood had destroyed, renewing the statutes and sacraments for the welfare of the people and the sacred land.

Harrappan Culture and the Indus Valley Civilization

The other great civilizations that were developing during this period were the Egyptian, Persian, and the Indus Valley civilization, which is located in modern Pakistan and India. Seals have been found in Sumer with Indus Valley script, which indicates trade and exchanges of technology and philosophy between these cultures. The Indus Valley civilization dates back at least to 3300 BCE in its earliest form but flowered in its mature period from 2600 –1900, roughly the same period as the Sumerian Renaissance and extending to the age of Abraham.

ABRAHAM AND THE ANCIENT WORLD | 21

The Indus Valley civilization, also known as the **Harrappan culture**, was spread out in the alluvial plains of the Indus River (what is now Pakistan) and flourished through agriculture and trade. The people of the Indus River were called the Indus people by the Persians. When Marco Polo came to this great river the Persian guides referred to them as the Indus people, which was pronounced Hindus by the Europeans, hence in the Western word Hindus and Hinduism refer to the people east of the great Indus River in the Indian subcontinent.

Evidence of the Harrappan culture exists in several sites along the old path of the Indus River that were discovered in 1922 by Rakhaldas Bandyopadhyay, an officer of the Archaeological Survey of India. He was led to a mound by a Buddhist monk who believed it might be a Buddhist stupa, or temple, only to find evidence of one of the world's greatest lost civilizations, much older than Buddha, on the grounds known as **Mohenjo-Daro**.

Mohenjo-Daro was built around 2600 BCE and abandoned around 1900 BCE. At its peak, it was the most developed and advanced city in South Asia and perhaps the world. Its streets were planned and laid out on a grid pattern, and its buildings were made of sun-dried brick and wood, and were up to two stories high—a technological achievement in its day. At its height, Mohenjo-Daro housed around 35,000 residents. There were public buildings and granaries, public baths, wells, and drains for waste water. They had a central marketplace and possibly heated water, while most of the world was still living in huts. They also excelled in art, making artifacts that expressed a wide range of movements and emotions, including, the dancing girl, the priest king and the sitting yogi.

The Harrappan script looks remarkably similar to Sumerian, although there are some distinct differences. The Harrappans had a system of uniform weights, measures, and time. They were a polytheistic culture, with a mother goddess, a supreme creator or sky god, and lesser deities. Shiva Lingams have been found on many of these sites, indicating the worship of Shiva. These distinctive phallic shaped stones, which are typically set on circular, woven pedestals, representing the union of the male and female energies, were some of the earliest know forms of worship in India.

One of the earliest names known for the Hindu god Shiva is **An**, the very same name as the Sumerian god of the heavens. According to K.C. Singhal in his book *The Ancient History of India* An appears in the world's oldest spiritual writing, the Indian Rig Veda, as well as in Hindu Puranas. In the Hindu epic the *Mahabharat* he is known as **Anu**. Both An and Anu refer to Shiva, the supreme godhead. Thus, the name and attributes of the Hindu god An are identical to those of the neighboring Sumerians' god An at the same time in history, and, thus, the almighty god of Abraham's civilization was apparently also the primordial god Shiva of the yogis.

One seal in particular is speculated to represent a proto-Shiva symbol believed to represent Pashupati (an epithet of Shiva). He sits cross-legged, similar to the famous yoga posture used for meditation, with bull horns on his head, similar to the Sumerian god of the heavens An. Also similar to Pashupati (Shiva), the sitting Harrappan yogi is surrounded by animals, as he is lord of the beasts. Furthermore, on one image there are several symbols running up and down the front of what looks like a yogi's body; these symbols are remarkably similar to the chakra symbols used by the yogis. The names, iconography, and meaning all lead us to speculate that both of these cultures shared similar spiritual beliefs and essentially recognized the same God—An.

We have better records of An from the Hindu culture. Shiva represents the divine in a state beyond form. He is the transcendent god, above all other gods, both the creator and destroyer of the universe who is beyond it. He is the known as the sky god, the creator of the universe, and father of mankind. He is the deity through whom the yogi aspires to attain enlightenment, and he is the destroyer of illusion, delusion, and error, so that one may attain it. He is also represented by the bull (Nandi) and is sometimes represented with bull horns on his head, similar to the Sumerian god An. He is the source of our eternal salvation through the realization of his divine presence within us and around us—enlightenment.

The Egyptian Civilization

Egypt is the other great civilization that was developing during biblical times. The history of Egypt is the longest continuous history of any country in the world. In what is known as the Upper Paleolithic region of Egypt, ancient tools and technologies were discovered that date back to 30,000 BCE. Grain harvesting and milling can be traced back to the Quran culture, which flourished along the Nile River around 10,000 BCE. The creation of the world's first state occurred in Egypt around 3000 BCE. In what is known as the Protodynastic Period, 3200-3000 BCE, ancient Egypt was undergoing a process of political unification with various city-states along the Nile. It was during this phase that the Egyptians developed hieroglyphs, another early form of writing.

It was during the Fourth Dynasty of Egypt, a period known as the golden age of the Old Kingdom, 2575 to 2467 BCE, that the pyramids were built, and Egypt prospered. Abraham lived during a period known as the Eleventh Dynasty of Egypt, which was based in Thebes under what is known as the Middle Kingdom. If Abraham lived around 2000 BCE, then one of the Mentuhotep Pharaohs was in power. During this time Egypt had extended its boundaries and sent expeditions to Phoenia (modern Lebanon) to obtain cedar. So, we know the Egyptians had a strong influence in Canaan during Abraham's time, and also that Abraham spent time in Egypt (Genesis 12:10).

The Egyptians were also polytheistic, with a plethora of gods and goddesses, but they were beginning to develop the idea of a supreme deity, a creator of heaven and earth, and developing the notions of an afterlife—a heaven and an underworld. Osiris, or Osiris <u>Ani</u>, is one of the oldest gods of Egypt, his name is written on the Palermo Stone, which dates back to about 2500 BCE. Osiris was the god of the afterlife. Egyptians sought eternity in a spiritual afterlife and believed in an underworld. There were also rules of conduct—commandments—that one had to observe to get into heaven. Osiris was a merciful god of judgment and the giver of life; he was associated with the Nile, and flooding and sprouting vegetation, and his creations were to obey him.

Horus was the son of the fertility goddess Isis and Osiris, and was known as the sky god. Horus had a man's body and a falcon's head, and the sun and the moon were within him—the sun was his right eye and the moon, his left. Horus rules, guides, and protects Egypt. Our access to immortality is attained through pleasing the gods and obeying the rules of conduct that were set forth by god in the world's oldest spiritual text found, known as the Pyramid Texts.

The Pyramid Texts are a collection of religious writings dating back 2400-2300 BCE, parts of which also appear in the Coffin Texts and the Book of the Dead, which came later. In the Pyramid Texts spells, chants, or mantras are given to enable the dead to ascend into heaven. Upon arrival it asserts that "The Gatekeeper comes out to you, he grasps your hand, takes you into heaven." In the Book of the Dead we are advised, and must convey to god before entering heaven, that we have not worshiped other gods, we have not lied, cheated, stolen, killed or injured others; essentially serving as the Egyptian equivalent of God's commandments.

Under the reign of Akhenaten (Amenhotep IV) from 1350 to 1330s BCE, Egypt became the first nation to create a state of monotheism. Aten, typically represented by the disk sun, was not to be tainted by the worshiping of other deities; he was the god of the heavens, god of creation, the one and only true God. Aten replaced all other gods; there was only one true God. Akhenaten built a new capital at Amarna, with a temple to Aten, but this early form of monotheism didn't last long, after the rein of Akhenaten, the old religion was restored.

Zoroastrianism

Another great monotheistic religion, Zoroastrianism, arose in Persia (modern Iran), swept through Sumerian lands, and spread into the entire Middle East; based on the teaching of the prophet **Zoroaster** or Zarathustra, Zoroastrianism is believed to date back to 8,000 BCE and possibly to the sixth century BCE. This religion first started to gain wide acceptance during the Achaemenid (Hakhamanian) Empire under Cyrus the Great, the first emperor of Persia around 600-529 BCE, but it remained obscure until Alexander the Great helped spread the teachings in the third century BCE after conquering Persia. It was generally replaced by Islam many centuries later. Zoroastrians continue to practice to this day in the Middle East, India (where they are known as Parsis), and the United States.

Zoroastrians were monotheists, they believed in the one creator god in heaven **Ahura Mazda**, and that Zoroaster was his prophet. Zoroastrians believe in heaven and hell, Satan, resurrection, and a final purification of the world. The religion's stories include a virgin birth, a savior of humanity, and the coming kingdom of heaven on earth. Zoroastrians believe that when we live by god's laws, we enter into heaven, and one day we will all live together in peace after being purified. Ahura Mazda is "the one Supreme God"...who is All Wise, All Good, and Eternal. Their priests were known as the Magi, and they are referred to in the nativity story of Christ (the Three Wise Men).

Zoroastrian writings are found amongst early Gnostic Christian works and in the Nag Hammadi Library, which will be discussed in greater length later. Thus, monotheistic theologies were well disseminated throughout the Middle East during the time of Abraham, and again during the time of Christ through an evolution of this religion known as **Mithraism**. The Hebrew accounts are still being passed down by oral tradition at this time, and we have no written Hebrew records until about the first century. Thus, during the first century there were several cultures developing the concept of one ultimate and supreme deity, an afterlife, and salvation. An awareness of there being one supreme deity was growing within the collective consciousness of humanity.

Ur

Ur was an ancient city-state in Sumer, in modern Tell el-Mukayyar in Iraq. Once a coastal city along the Euphrates River, with its mouth on the Persian Gulf, over the years silt deposits have extended the land so that it is now well inland of the ocean. Central to Ur was the ziggurat temple to the moon goddess Nanna (or sin). This stepped brick structure rises seventy feet like a pyramid, but it is now flat on top; it was built around 2100 BCE during the reign of Ur-Nammu. Ur was favorably located for trade by both sea and land; whoever became king of Ur became king of Sumer.

The Third Dynasty of Ur under king Ur-Nammu set forth the famous laws, or Code of Ur-Nammu, which is the first record of law in history, predating the code of Hammurabi by 300 years. During the time of Abraham, Ur was considered the largest city in the world and had a population of over 65,000. This period was followed by a major shift in population, as people migrated from southern Iraq toward the north and west, along roughly the same path that Abraham followed; so Abraham was not likely the first Hebrew to migrate from Mesopotamia to the Levant. Other Semite groups had already settled in Canaan at least centuries earlier.

During the Ur III period there was an apparent problem with soil salinity, making agriculture less productive and necessitating a shift from growing wheat to the more salt-tolerant barley. So, in Abraham's time making a living off the land was becoming increasingly more difficult, and people were forced to migrate. It is estimated that during this time the population declined by nearly three-fifths. There was mass migration and increased competition for land. Moreover, in 1940 BCE the Elamites invaded Ur and sacked it, which gave rise to Amorite rule that ended with the rise of Babylonia under Hammurabi in 1700 BCE. So the Hebrews had good reason for migrating during Abraham's time. It was during this time that Abraham hears God tell him (Genesis 12:1):

> **Get thee out of thy country and from thy kindered, and from thy father's house, unto a land that I will show thee.**

The Migration of Abraham

Abraham (Abram) leaves his family in Ur and migrates to Haran, which is believed to be the classical Carrhae, which lies along the Balikh River, a branch of the Euphrates, now eastern Turkey. After a short stay, Abraham and his new wife, Sarah (Sarai), along with his nephew Lot (the son of Abraham's brother), went to Canaan. In Genesis God tells Abraham to go to "the land I will show you", and promised to bless him. So Abraham takes his family and heads south to Canaan to start a new life and create a blessed group of people - his progeny.

Canaan is the ancient term for the region encompassing modern day Palestine, Israel, and Lebanon, as well as parts of Jordan, Syria, and northeastern Egypt; it is also referred to as the Holy Land, the Promised Land, or Zion. The Canaanites spoke a western Semitic language and are referred to in the Bible, as well as in Mesopotamian and Egyptian texts. According to Eblaite scholars the name Canaan (ga-na-na), dates back to 2350 BCE. Canaanites engaged in trade with the Egyptian, Sumerian, and Minoan Crete cultures from before the Bronze Age. The culture was very much tied to the sea. The mythology of Canaan, and its ties to the sea are illustrated in the struggles between the Canaanite gods Ba'al (Teshub), the god of storms, and Ya'a (Yaw, Yahu or Yam), the god of the sea. Ba'al is mentioned over sixty times in the Bible, and the attributes of both these deities becomes absorbed into the Hebrew monotheistic concept of God.

Early ethnic groups occupying Canaan included Philistine, Phoenician, Hurrians, Hittites, Aramaeans, Moabites, and Ammonites, as well as, Hebrews. This land, or parts of it, were under Egyptian rule on and off through much of its early history. In the centuries preceding the appearance of the biblical Hebrews, Canaan became a tributary to the Egyptian Pharaohs, with frequent local rebellions breaking out. In Genesis (10:15-19) in what is called the Table of Nations, Canaanites are described as being descended from an ancestor called Canaan, who was the son of Ham (Noah's son). Thus, by biblical tradition the Canaanites were descendents of Noah and, thereby, common ancestors of Abraham and part of his extended family.

The Canaanite God El

The Canaanites were polytheistic, but their principal god was El, also known in Canaan by the names: Eli, Al, iah, Yah Eli, or Izer, which are Semite for *power* or *all powerful*. The word *Eli* was found at the top of a list of gods in the ruins of the Elba civilization, at the Tell Mardikh archaeological site in modern Syria, which dates back to 2300 BCE. El is also husband to the fertility goddess **Asherah**, who had been worshiped by Hebrews for centuries and is mentioned over forty times in the Old Testament. When the Hebrews first came to Canaan, they worshiped El and Asherah. This supreme deity introduces himself to Abraham in Genesis as **El Shaddai** or Lord of the Mountain, which is one of his Canaanite titles. We also see this name preserved in names of places, such as, Beth-*el* or Isra-*el*, and in names such as Ishma-*el* or *El*-ohim.

Another Semite group called the Hurrian refer to God as both El of the Covenant and El the Judge respectively. El is also spelled *Al* in Arabic and becomes Al-lah or Allah (the God) to the Arab people; Muslims recognize Al and El as the same one almighty God, the same God of the Jews and Christians. Islam's prophet, Mohammad, studied Christianity with his uncle who was a Christian, and he believed in the same God as the Christians and Jews. El is also known as Toru El (Bull El or the bull god) and is often represented by a bull or calf, similar to the Sumerian An. That is why Moses found the Hebrews worshiping a golden calf when he came down from Mount Sinai; that is the symbol of El the god they worshiped. In the Sumerian language God is **An**, in the Semite language of the Akkadians it's **Anu**, in the Semite language of Arabic it's **Al** or Allah, and in Canaanite and Hebrew it's **El**. An, Al, and El are the same transcendent God.

In the Bible El is sometimes used generically to refer to god or gods and might include Ba'<u>al</u> or Yahweh, and at other times it is used more poetically. He is referred to 217 times in the Masoretic text, 73 times in the Psalms and 55 times in the Book of Job (referring to the God), and other times as a foreign god, as in Deuteronomy (32:12) and Malachi (2:11), and is gradually replaced by name **Yahweh** (YHWH) from the time of Moses on. Note, *Ya* or *Yah* is yet another name for El. In Exodus (6:2-3) Yahweh tells Moses: "I revealed myself to Abraham, to Isaac, and to Jacob as El Shaddai, but was not known to them by my name Yahweh." As El was also known as El Shaddai, or Lord of the Mountain, it was natural for Moses to climb Mount Sinai to commune with his god.

In *The Oxford Companion to World Mythology*, David Leeming asserts that "it seems almost certain that the God of the Jews evolved gradually from the Canaanite El, who was in all likelihood the 'God of Abraham.'" Moreover, in Karen Armstrong's best seller *A History of God* she concludes, "It is highly likely that Abraham's God was El, the High God of Canaan." From the time of Moses on we see a transition from *El* to *Yahweh* being used to represent the supreme god. Psalm 29 states "Ascribe to Yahweh, sons of gods. Ascribe to Yahweh, glory and strength," and in Psalm 89:6 we find, "For who in the skies compares to Yahweh, who can be likened to Yahweh among the sons of gods." In Exodus (15.11): "Who is like you among the gods, Yahweh?" So we can clearly see evidence of the evolution of God within Judaism from being first amongst gods to being the one and only true God of all people and places.

We also see an evolution of God from being a personal god with whom you can make personal contact and who appears in human, and other, forms, to being transcendental. He comes to Abraham as a friend. El gives friendly advice and guides the Hebrews in their wanderings, advising them who to marry and coming to them in dreams. He even comes in human form, an idea that would later become blasphemous in Judaism. In Genesis (18) we are told that God (El) appeared to Abraham by the oak tree of Mamre, near Hebron. Abraham looks up and sees three strangers approaching his tent and invites them to sit and rest while Sarah prepares food for them. During the conversation, it is revealed that one of the three men is actually God in human form, and the other two turn out to be angels.

As the Israelites (Hebrews) mixed with Canaanite and other cultures in the Levant, they also adapted and adopted much of the theology of the land. Throughout the Bible, there are instances of prophets warning their people not to worship other gods but for hundreds of years Israelites continued to worship El, Ba'al, and the goddess Asherah. Even the columns to the temple that Solomon built for Yahweh were in honor of and in the style of Jewish goddess worship. People believed Asherah was Yahweh's wife. During this time period, animal sacrifice was the primary form of worship. After Moses, the attributes of all these deities rolled into the one almighty god—Yahweh. Yahweh became so big you could not see him, you could not touch him, and you could not even utter his name. He is beyond form, beyond description, beyond the comprehension. He became transcendental in their eyes, and worshiping the old gods became punishable by death.

Abraham's Journey

God promises to show Abraham a land where he can be fruitful and multiply, but the land is barren and dry and the people are hostile. He and his family are forced to flee this Promised Land and seek refuge in Egypt (Genesis 12:10-20). Fearing that the pharaoh had evil designs that jeopardized his life and knowing that the pharaoh would find his wife, Sarah, beautiful, Abraham sells Sarah to the pharaoh in exchange for herds and slaves. Sarah then becomes a part of the pharaoh's harem. It was a common practice for Semitic chiefs to be married to their half-sisters to retain property within the family, and Abraham explains that Sarah is his sister, a half-sister on his father's side.

When the pharaoh finds out the plagues on his nation are the result of him marrying Abraham's wife, the pharaoh sends them all on their way, and they head back to Canaan, with their new herds and slaves. Abraham, Sarah, and Lot return to a place called Ali in Canaan to homestead, but conflict over land and water soon arises between Abraham's and Lot's herdsmen. So they agree to split up to ensure they'll each have enough land and water for their herds to graze. Lot picks the land east of the Jordan River and Abraham moved down to the oaks of Mamre in Hebron, after receiving another promise from El that his progeny should be as numerous as the stars in heaven.

After rescuing his nephew Lot from the hands of Chedorlaomer, who had raided Lot's tribe and taken Lot prisoner, Abraham meets with the great king and priest of Salem (Jerusalem) **Melchizedek**. It is through Melchizedek that Abraham is offered blessed bread and wine as part of a sacrament on Abraham's behalf. So we see that at the same time the Hebrews were homesteading in Canaan, Abraham's people were adopting Canaanite rites and rituals. Still, Abraham had no heirs despite God's promise, so, in accordance with the custom of the time, Sarah gives Abraham Hagar, Sarah's new slave girl from Egypt, with whom to propagate.

Hagar has a son, Ishmael, who Abraham is quite proud of, but Sarah becomes very jealous and starts mistreating Hagar. After finally giving birth to her own son, **Isaac**, Sarah pressures Abraham to banish Hagar and Ishmael, and leave them to fend for themselves. Now Isaac becomes the undisputed heir, but first there is a test of Abraham's loyalty to God. After raising Isaac to be a young man, God commands Abraham (he believes) to offer his son Isaac up as a burnt offering or human sacrifice (Genesis 22:6). (Human sacrifice was still common in Canaan at this time). Fortunately, at the last minute, God sends an angel who grabs Abraham's arm and keeps him from finishing the task. Anxious to fulfill the vision of multitudes of his people propagating and flourishing, Abraham sends Isaac's steward, Eliezer, back to Mesopotamia to find an appropriate Hebrew wife for Isaac.

Eliezer returns with Rebekah, daughter of Bethuel, granddaughter of Nahor, and, consequently, Abraham's niece, and Isaac's first-cousin (Genesis 24:14-16). After Sarah dies at the age of 127, Abraham takes another wife who bears him six more sons: Zimran, Jokshan, Medan, Midian, Ishbak, and Shuah (Genesis 24:1-6). Abraham dies at the age of 175, with eight sons to carry his lineage, but it is only through Isaac that our biblical story continues. After twenty years of marriage to Isaac, Rebekah gives birth to twin boys, Esau and **Jacob**. As a young man, Jacob tricks his now blind, aging father into giving him the blessings and estate of his father over his elder brother Esau. Jacob ends up doing quite well and has twelve sons and one daughter through his two wives Leah, Rachel, and through their maidservants, Bilhah and Zilpah.

Patriarchs and Prophets

The patriarchal lineage runs from Abraham, to his son Isaac, and to Isaac's son Jacob. Jacob's sons are Reuben, Simeon, Levi, Judah, Dan, Naphtali, Gad, Asher, Issachar, Zebulum, Joseph, and Benjamin; his daughter is Dinah. These twelve male descendents become known as the children of Israel, the forefathers of the twelve tribes of Israel. While traveling to Harah, Jacob experiences a vision in which he sees a ladder reaching into heaven with angels going up and down it—Jacob's Ladder. From the top he hears a voice from God, who bestows many blessings on him. Later, while traveling to meet his brother Esau, who is seeking revenge for being cheated out of the family estate, Jacob spends the night in the desert in communion with God and a mysterious being appears to Jacob. In Genesis (32:24) this being is described as "a man" and in Hosea (12:4) as "an angel." Jacob wrestles with this apparent emissary of God all night and finally subdues him. Jacob then demands a blessing whereupon this mystical being declares that from now on Jacob will be called Israel, meaning one who has prevailed with God (El).

Afterward Jacob names this place Pnei-*el*, meaning "face of God," stating "I have seen God face to face and lived." From this time on the Holy Land is called Israel, and the descendents of Jacob are known as the Israelites. Jacob makes up with his brother Esau, but Jacob's sons are so jealous of their bother **Joseph** that they sell him as a slave to a caravan headed for Egypt, where he is sold to a rich Egyptian (Genesis 37:28). Joseph, being brighter than average, enables his Egyptian master to prosper greatly and rises in the ranks of slaves. He also helps interpret a dream that was plaguing the pharaoh, and when his interpretation is fulfilled and Joseph's suggestions keep Egypt from starvation, the pharaoh promotes Joseph to top secretary over all food production and storage. He essentially becomes the pharaoh's minister of agriculture.

Drought then seizes Israel, and Joseph's brother's journey to Egypt to buy food, not knowing that their little brother became an Egyptian slave or that he now occupied a high position in Egypt. As a grown man in Egyptian garb, Joseph's brothers don't recognize him. After testing his brothers, Joseph eventually reveals who he is and invites his whole family to join him, which they do. Now the other descendents of Abraham and Isaac remain in Canaan, while the descendents of Jacob go to live in Egypt and are eventually enslaved by the Egyptians. For generations they lived under Egyptian rule, until a leader arose to take them back to the Promised Land. That leader was Moses.

Moses

According to the book of Exodus, Moses was born to a Hebrew -mother, Jochebed, who protected him when the pharaoh had ordered the killing of all newborn Hebrew boys because it was believed a threat to his crown would be born among the Hebrews. She placed him in a basket and floated him down the Nile, and he was picked up and adopted by the pharaoh's daughter and became a part of the pharaoh's family. So Moses was raised in a privileged class and would have been afforded an education—an Egyptian education. In Acts 7:22 Christ's disciple Stephen tells the Jewish Council in Jerusalem that was judging him "And Moses was learned in all the wisdom of the Egyptians, and was mighty in words and deeds." After killing an Egyptian slave master for mistreating a Hebrew slave, Moses at first fled from the law but later returned with instructions from God to lead his people out of Egypt and back to the Promised Land of Israel.

Moses's God sent ten plagues, including frogs, gnats, flies, diseases, boils, hail, locusts, and total darkness on the Egyptians. After the pharaoh unsuccessfully tried to have all firstborn Hebrew males slain (an event celebrated as the Passover because the angel of death "passed over" the Hebrew boys), the pharaoh finally allowed the Hebrews to leave but quickly changed his mind. While on their way back to Canaan, which lies to the north, the pharaoh sent his troops after them to bring them back, but the Israelites were already crossing the marshlands on route to Canaan that are known as the **Sea of Reeds** or the **Reed Sea.** It is important to note that contrary to popular belief, Moses did not cross the Red Sea, which is many hundreds of miles farther away and in a completely different direction than Canaan. A translation error led us to think it was the Red Sea. These were the marshy areas where the papyrus grows that were prone to flooding. After the Israelites had already crossed, the estuary began flooding; whether from rivers swollen from rain or a tidal action we don't know, but some natural act of God precluded the pharaoh's army from catching them, and the Israelites were at last free. However, since Canaan was already settled by other ethnic groups, the Israelites were forced to wander the desert for the next forty years.

It is during this time in the desert that Moses begins to reform the religion of the Hebrews and consolidates his leadership amongst his people. Having been the pharaoh's adopted son, he would naturally have developed leadership skills and developed his mind. We don't know how much Moses studied the traditions of the Hebrews, but it appears that he studied Egyptian philosophy while in Egypt. As death and the afterlife were an integral part of Egyptian life, especially for royalty, Moses would certainly have been familiar with the Pyramid Text and Egyptian Book of the Dead. These books outlined the Egyptian spiritual precepts that we recognize as God's commandments (Section 125 The Declaration of Innocence). These were new ideas to the Israelites, but they were already common beliefs within the Egyptian culture.

So it appears that Moses was able to take these Egyptian values and commandments like revering God, not cursing God, and not committing murder, have intercourse with a married woman, bare false witness, steal, cheat, covet, etc. and introduces these concepts to the Hebrews when he came down from Mount Sinai. He also reveals that the one true god is not El or Ba'al or any other god but the one supreme god Yahweh and that the traditional worship of other gods would no longer be tolerated. When Moses comes down from the mountain he finds his Israelite tribesmen worshiping their traditional god El in its traditional form of a calf. This infuriates Moses, and it is from this point on in our biblical history that we see Yahweh struggle to retain supremacy over other gods within the houses of Israel. We also see the god of the Israelites evolve from being a tribal and local god to being the one and only God—monotheism.

Yahweh is a jealous God. To worship another god was punishable by death (Exodus 32). Yahweh was also a god of war. One of the first acts of Yahweh, according to the Bible, was genocide. After wandering in the desert for forty years **Joshua**, who leads the Israelites after Moses dies, begins by laying siege to an unsuspecting city-state of Jericho. He believes that God has given him the mandate "to kill every man, woman and child" and take their possessions (Joshua 6: 21). Under Joshua's leadership the Israelites continued to sweep through Israel, killing every man, woman and child (Joshua 8:12, Numbers 26:51, Deuteronomy 2, 3, and 7). Over sixty cities, towns, and villages were completely destroyed; historians estimate that up to as many as six million people were massacred over the coming years—it was a holocaust.

Prisoners were rounded up and beheaded until the Israelites had complete control. But if all the people who inhabited Israel were killed as the Bible states, wouldn't that also include the other Hebrew tribes? Are not Esau's and Joseph's brothers', descendents still living in Israel? What about the descendents of Lot? Abraham took another wife after Sarah died and had six more sons (Genesis 24:1-6): Zimran, Jokshan, Medan, Midian, Ishbak, and Shuah. Apparently, their descendents were included in the slaughter. After this conquest, the Israelite tribes began fighting among themselves. After years of tribal infighting, the prophet Samuel picked **Saul** to be the first king of Israel, but **David** came forward as the natural leader after making a name for himself by killing the pillaging giant Goliath and other rival kings; it was under David that all the tribes came together to create one united kingdom.

King David (900 BC) is the hero of the Israelites, the one who unites his people and brings them pride and repute. But as blood is on his hands from all his killing, it is left to David's son **Solomon** to build the great temple to Yahweh, which he does, and it becomes famous throughout the lands. But the new nation of Israel is quickly divided into the state of Israel to the north and Judea to the south. These kingdoms expanded and contracted for several generations as they fought with the Philistines and other tribes but were then conquered and taken captive by the Assyrians (800-500 BC). King Josiah (700-600 BC) was able to unite the Israelites, and during this brief period they restored the law, but then the Babylonians invaded (600-500 BC) and subjugated the Israelites under King Nebacanezzer of Babylon. It was during this time that the great temple to Yahweh in Jerusalem was destroyed. The Israelites believed Yahweh was punishing them for worshiping other gods, but he was with them while they were living in servitude in Babylon. The Hebrews kept their culture alive by reading the Torah together as families, rather than by having traditional animal sacrifices at a temple. Under Cyrus the Great of Persia in 537 BCE, the Israelites were allowed to go back to Israel and to rebuild their temple, which they did. The Israelites begin migrating back to Israel, and they managed to carry on despite being repeatedly conquest by many foreign nations over the next few hundred years.

In addition to being influenced by the Sumerians, Canaanites, and Egyptians early on, after Alexander the Great conquered the Persian Emperor Darius and then the whole Middle East, Greek culture began to spread and every quarter of this new realm became Hellenized. Then the Romans began conquering the known world about a hundred years before Christ. By the time of Christ, Greco-Roman influences dominated every facet of civilization. So in this next chapter we are going to look at conditions leading up to and existing at the time of Christ's birth. It was an exciting time, with a lot of new ideas and new groups, and there was an awakening of consciousness. In the face of so much war and oppression, the Israelites turned to Yahweh for salvation, for he was also a merciful god who would send them a messiah.

• • •

Judaism and the Messiah

The time leading up to the birth of Jesus Christ was a time of religious fervor for the Jews, with various competing sects called the Pharisees, the Sadducees, the Zealots, and the Essenes vying to be the voice of Judaism. It was a time of mysticism, with the influences of Jewish Kabballah, Egyptian Hermetic, and Mithran cults, as well as Greeks like Socrates, Plato, Aristotle, the Epicureans, and the Stoics. The Romans had the Jews under their yoke, and the Jews turned to religion for hope. Some groups were expecting a Messiah any day, but they weren't looking for someone who could raise the dead, heal people, or walk on water, they were looking for a righteous king who would deliver them from Roman rule and re-establish their state of Israel. Caesar was like a foreign god usurping Yahweh's dominion. They needed hope, and they needed a leader. They needed a messiah.

The Persians conquered Babylon in 539 BCE and in 537 BCE, Cyrus the Great allowed the Jews to return to Israel, after living as slaves under the Babylonians for generations. They were also allowed to rebuild their temple in 515 BCE but were not allowed a monarchy, which put the temple priests in power. These temple priests become known as the **Sadducees**. By the first century the Sadducees came to represent the more orthodox and conservative; they were of the elite and priestly cast going back to Zadok (the high priest of Solomon's temple). This was also a time of creating the Jewish canon by the Sanhedrin (an assembly of priests) that became known as the written Torah or Hebrew Bible. They also created the oral Torah known as the Talmud. Years of living abroad compelled the Israelites to create a clear and common law and liturgy that would bring them together as a people. Judaism was still evolving its theology, and many new schools of thought were emerging during this time.

The **Pharisees** were at various times a political party, a separatist movement, and a school of thought that flourished during the Second Temple Era (536 BCE–70 CE); they were similar to the protestants of Christianity in that they questioned the authority of the established temple priests and that they favored the independent, or small group study, of the Torah and believed that all children of Israel should be knowledgeable of God's word. During their years in exile in Babylon the Jews did not have a temple to attend, so Jewish houses of assembly, known as *beit Knesset* (in Greek, synagogue), became the meeting place for prayer. Instead of priests reading the Torah, patriarchal elders would read it out loud to their extended families. This kept the religion alive and led to a populous movement among the people of Israel; this also led to greater openness to new ideas and the development of a higher consciousness as they began questioning the meaning of these biblical stories.

Pharisees also believed in the written Torah and the Talmud, the oral Torah. The sages of the Talmud believed that the oral Torah was not a fixed text but an ongoing process of analysis and argument. They believed such argument, discussion, and questioning allowed God to guide them; they also believed that God was actually involved in their questioning and that they were participating in God's ongoing revelation. The Pharisees believed in the resurrection of the dead and in a messianic age, contrary to the Sadducees. The Pharisees were gaining in popularity and importance by the time of Christ and set forth the changes that help create other Jewish groups, such as the Zealots and the Essenes. They were also believed to be the forerunners of Rabbinical Judaism as practiced today. During this time we see a movement away from animal sacrifices at the temple to study and debate of the law and teachings of the Torah that was being canonized around this time.

The **Zealots** were a group of revolutionaries whose aim was to kick the Romans out of Israel. But the last of the Zealots killed themselves in an apparent mass suicide during their final stand against the Romans at the great fortress of Masada in 73 CE. The Essenes are a particularly interesting group of Jews that were apparently tied very closely to the Jesus movement, so we will take some time getting to understand them better.

The Essenes

What we know of the Essenes comes from Roman historians, from the church fathers, and later from the **Dead Sea Scrolls** that are generally attributed to be from an Essene community in Qumran, along the Dead Sea, in Israel. The Jewish philosopher **Philo** of Alexandra (20–54 CE) mentions the Essenes in his *Hypothetica* and claims there are "more than four thousand" of them; the Roman historian **Pliny** the Elder locates them in the desert near the Dead Sea, which gives further credence to the Dead Sea Scrolls being of Essene origin. We learn the most about the Essenes through Josephus and his two books from the first century, *The Jewish War* and *Antiquities of the Jews*.

Flavius Josephus (37–100 CE) was born Yosef Ben Matiyahu, an ethnic Jew and a priest from Jerusalem, who served as a military leader during the revolts against the Romans in Galilee. After the Jewish garrison of Yodfat fell to the Romans under Flavius Vespasian and his son Titus, Josephus surrendered and was taken prisoner. It is believed that Josephus predicted Vespasian's rise to Caesar, which seemed unlikely at the time since Vespasian was not of royal Roman blood. But when it came to pass that, apparently, this put Yosef in good terms with Vespasian, who invited him to Rome. Yosef then left for Rome with Vespasian's son, Titus, and became a Roman citizen. He then changed his name to Flavius (Vespasian's family name) Josephus (Yosef) and became Caesar's historian, writing first *The Jewish War* and then *Antiquities of the Jews* during the first century.

One of the most significant contributions to history Josephus makes is in his familiarity with Jesus Christ. Josephus is the only non biblical source that speaks about Jesus as if he had met or heard him and was familiar with his character. He has great respect for Jesus and his ministering and healing, but does not consider him to be the Messiah. Many historians also question Josephus' mention of Christ's ascension, as that passage is written in a different style and appears to have been added years later, but this single brief section suggests we have independent evidence that a physical Jesus did, in fact, exist; albeit as more of a prophet than a god or the Messiah of the Jews. In his *Antiquities of the Jews* Joseph states:

> Now, there was about this time, Jesus, a wise man, if it be lawful to call him a man, for he was a doer of wonderful works, - a teacher of such men as receive the truth with pleasure. He drew over to him both many of the Jews, and many of the Gentiles.

The Essenes were a Jewish sect that broke away from the mainstream and existed during the second century BCE to the first century CE; the term is also used broadly to refer to the many fringe groups that were developing during the first century. They were mystical, messianic, and ascetic and shunned the temples of their forefathers. Although not an Essene, Josephus respects the Essenes for their efforts to be pious and sincere in their practices. Most sects were celibate and lived a communal life like the early Christians. They were forbidden from swearing oaths, making animal sacrifices, or criminal or immoral activities. They had collective ownership, could not hold slaves, and they served each other as a very tight knit community. They were also peace activists awaiting the Messiah to bring about the kingdom of heaven on earth.

One of most interesting attributes of the Essenes was their ritual rite of purification through **baptisms**. Whereas Jews would wash themselves before entering the temple, the Essenes were unique in that they would change into white garments and immerse themselves in water to cleanse themselves before prayers and breaking bread together. Because this was the custom of John the Baptist many scholars believe that John the Baptist (and perhaps even Jesus as he was baptized by John) may have been part of the community. It is likely that the Essenes were among the first Jews to follow Jesus and that the first Christians had adopted their Essene ways and lifestyle. The Essenes also believed that man had a spiritual nature within his mortal flesh that was his true nature. They believed our purpose was to purify the body and mind for use of the spirit. Josephus describes their philosophy as follows:

> That bodies are corruptible, and that the matter they are made of is not permanent; but that the souls are immortal, and continue forever; and that they come out of the most subtle air, and are united to their bodies as in prisons, into which they are drawn by certain natural enticement; but that when they are set free from the bonds of the flesh, they then, as released from a long bondage, rejoice and mount upward.

So we see in the Essenes a movement away from the traditional rites of animal sacrifice and authority of the priesthood, to a seeking of their internal, eternal nature as spirit. They endeavored to develop their body and mind to become purer vehicles for the spirit to guide them. This philosophy and spiritual training has more in common with the yogis of India and the Buddhists of the Himalayas, and the esoteric Kabbalah teachings of the Jews, than the orthodox Jewish theology of its day. Moreover, these ideas are expressed in the writings of the Dead Sea Scrolls, which we visit next.

The Dead Sea Scrolls

The Dead Sea Scrolls were discovered between 1947 and 1956 in eleven caves in and around Wadi **Qumran**, Israel, near the ruins of an ancient settlement believed to be Essene. The caves are above the Dead Sea, hence the scrolls' name. These manuscripts date from 150 BCE to 70 CE and include some 800 scrolls, the only known surviving copies of biblical documents made before 100 CE. The Dead Sea Scrolls contain versions of the Hebrew Bible (before it was canonized), as well as other books not included in the Old Testament. Before their discovery, the oldest known versions of the Old Testament dated back to the fourth century CE, but the Dead Sea Scrolls date back to the second century BCE. The earliest copies of the Old Testament were in Greek manuscripts such as Codex Vaticanus and Codex Sinaiticus, whereas the Dead Sea Scrolls are in Hebrew and Aramaic (native languages), as well as Greek.

What has been published of the Dead Sea Scrolls shows a remarkable diversity of thought and shows variances in interpretation of scripture. Moreover, the Dead Sea Scrolls also include apocryphal writings not seen before. According to Robert Eisenman in *his The Dead Sea Scrolls Uncovered*, these works were "Messianic, visionary and mystical—even Kabbalistic." New themes appear in these pieces of parchment and papyrus, including God's "Spirit hovering over the Meek" and "announcing glad tiding to the Meek" and how the pious will be "glorified on the Throne of the Eternal Kingdom," which sounds more like New Testament writing than the Old Testament, indicating a new direction in thinking. The following excerpts prove helpful.

The Messiah of Heaven and Earth (4Q521) plate 1, fragment 1 column 2, it states:

> The Heavens and earth will obey His Messiah ...and all that is in them. He will not turn aside from the Commandments of the Holy Ones. Take strength in His service, (you) who seek the Lord. Shall you not find the Lord in this, all of you who wait patiently in your hearts? For the Lord will visit the Pious Ones and the righteous will He call by name. Over the meek will His Spirit hover, and the faithful will He restore by His power. He shall glorify the Pious Ones on the throne of the Eternal Kingdom.

The Dead Sea Scrolls also speak in a language similar to the Gnostic literature of the first Jewish followers of Jesus, referring to spiritual ascents or journeys, "knowing the mysteries" and having "secret inner knowledge". Moreover, the references to knowing are often in the feminine (she), similar to how the first century Christians referred to this inner knowledge as *Sophia* (from the Greek). The Dead Sea Scrolls also includes pieces of horoscopes, indicating their interest in and use of astrology, and knowledge of the signs and ages. What makes these Jews different from the ones who go to temple regularly is that they take it on themselves to interpret the scriptures for themselves and look for an awakening of knowledge or *gnosis* from within.

The Demons of Death (4Q525) plate 12, column 2, the spiritual aspirant is instructed as follows:

> And now, understand, hear me, and set your heart to [do as follows]. Bring forth the Knowledge of your inner self and meditate.

Note the emphasis on meditation and introspection; we are to look for something within ourselves. The answers lie within us. As we look within and meditate, we raise our consciousness, and we become more enlightened. In the next sentence we receive further instruction:

> In the Meekness of Righteousness bring forth [your] words in order to give them...[don't] respond to the words of your neighbor lest he give you [permission?]. As you hear, answer accordingly.

These first-century Jews and Christians were taught to be mindful and take conscious control of their thoughts, words, and actions. They were looking for an inner knowing, a realization of their own eternal nature and God. In The Birth of Noah (4Q534-536) fragment 2, column 1, we are told how the Lord will "reveal Mysteries like the Highest Angels" and gain "Understanding of the Mysteries." One of the best examples of the development of Gnostic thinking within the Jewish community comes from a scroll called The Book of Secrets, in which man is encouraged to look within and to think for himself:

The Book of Secrets (4Q299) fragment 8, it is written:

> How can a man understand without knowledge or hearing? He created insight for His children, by much wisdom He uncovered our ears that we might hear. He created insight for all those who pursue true knowledge (Gnosis) and all wisdom is from eternity.

So the Essene groups clearly were moving monotheism to a more contemplative and introspective theology—a more mystical and meditative path to God. But they were not the only ones. There is a whole corpus of literature referred to as Pseudepigrapha that refers to Jewish apocalyptic literature and testaments written from 200 BCE to 200 CE. Pseudepigraphic works refer to works whose author attributed it to a figure in the past, such as the *Odes of Solomon*. It is not likely The Odes were actually written by King Solomon but was instead inspired writings based on this historical figure. These works also tend to be called Apocrypha as they are spiritual texts that fall outside the historical canon of the Old or New Testaments.

Jewish Apocrypha and Pseudepigrapha

The Apocrypha are the secret writings that were rejected for liturgical public reading either because the Church authorities thought the material would confuse congregations or that the material was unclear in there meaning or authenticity, or because the material was considered spurious, contentious, or false. Many of these books appear in the Septuagint (Greek) and the Vulgate (Latin) or ancient versions but not in the modern Hebrew Bible or in the Protestant Bibles. Catholic's sometimes refer to such texts as deuterocanonical. Sometimes referred to as the lost books of the Bible; examples of Old Testament Pseudepigrapha are the Ethiopian Book of Enoch, Jubilees, 4 Ezra, and The Life of Adam and Eve.

In these lost books of the Old Testament, we also receive more information about the Messiah. In 4 Ezra the Messiah is depicted like a great Davidic king, a "Lion" who will denounce, judge, and destroy the ungodly and deliver the faithful. Also in 4 Ezra, we hear about the prophesy:

> The Messiah, who is "my son" and "a man" withstands a warring multitude and consumes them with "a stream of fire" that proceeds from his mouth.

The Messiah is God's son, but he is a man. He is not a god or of the same substance of God; he is a man. First and foremost he is the leader of the Israelites, and the one who will destroy their oppressors and rule righteously under God's law. Mankind seems to be constantly tested and challenged and keeps breaking God's laws and making mistakes, which is all part of mankind's evolution to higher consciousness—the growing up pains of a consciousness enlightening.

In this age, there is no original sin, in the sense of mankind being tainted because Adam and Eve disobeyed God. The concept of original sin is foreign to Judaism and early Christianity, — its origins are pagan. Man sins by not listening to Yahweh or obeying his laws; mankind, and God's chosen people in particular, keeps making mistakes in God's eyes and are punished for their sins and rewarded for their righteousness. One of the most interesting stories that refer to sin on earth appears in the **Book of Enoch** (1 Enoch 6:1-2) describing the fall of angles:

> In those days, when the children of man had multiplied, it happened that there were born unto them handsome and beautiful daughters. And the Angels, the children of heaven, saw them and desired them; and they said to one another, "Come, let us choose wives for ourselves from among the daughters of man and beget us children."

And so they did. The angels not only had sex with the women, they had giant children by them. The angels also taught the women "magical medicine, incantations, the cutting of roots, and plants." We also see a correlation to acts of sex and a loss of innocence that brings about bad character in God's eyes. This cavorting led to acts of adultery and bloodshed and the Angels Michael, Surafel, and Gabriel went up to heaven and told God about this, and God was so disgusted that he destroyed everyone by a deluge.

The Merkabah

In 3 Enoch we have an account of how Enoch journeyed to heaven, saw God's throne and chariot, received revelations from the Archangel Metatron, and viewed the wonders of the upper world. Through the mystical Jewish teachings of Merkabah, God is revealed; fasting and the invocation of YHWH (God's name) or the archangels by their holy names with a rhythmic repetition of certain words or sounds, like a mantra, enable the practitioner to ascend to heavenly states or realms. There are seven inner realms and in the center lies the Merkabah—Yahweh's throne.

The Merkabah texts concentrate on the mysteries of heaven and the description of God's throne. There are worlds within worlds within themselves that the aspirant goes through in his search for God. Of course, the symbolism is a metaphor and the journey is within. As is the case with all the Old Testament scripture, the biblical stories provide lessons about life that we are to learn from and are not to be taken literally (although the actual incidents are believed to have taken place).

In The Book of Enoch:

> "When I ascended to the height to behold the vision of the chariot, I entered six palaces, one inside the other, and when I reached the door of the seventh palace I paused in prayer before the Holy One, blessed be he; I looked up and said: Lord of the Universe, grant, I beseech you, that the merit of Aaron son of Amram, lover of peace and pursuer of peace, who received on Mount Sinai the crown of priesthood in the presence of your glory, may avail for me now, so that Prince Qaspi'el (an Angel and gatekeeper of the sixth palace), and the angels with him not prevail over me and chase me from heaven.

Then the angel Metatron, the "Prince of the Divine Presence," grasps him and takes him into the presence of the "high and most exalted King" to behold the likeness of the chariot. He goes on to say "Then I entered the seventh palace and he led me to a camp of the Sekinah (rough equivalent is *spirit*) and presented me before the throne of glory so that I might behold the chariot." The chariot is often symbolically used to represent the vehicle; this is a metaphysical message describing an inner journey to realize God. The light from the presence of the seraphim and cherubim (high and low angels) was so bright that they were ordered to "hide their eyes" from the earthling so they wouldn't tremble, and Metatron has to lift Enoch back to his feet after being overwhelmed and falling to his knees from the awesomeness of it all.

Then God reveals the great secrets to Enoch: "All the mysteries of the world and all the orders of nature stand revealed before me as they stand revealed before the Creator." A crown is then placed on his head (symbolizing transcendence) and he is introduced to the angels who guide the world, and they all fell prostrate before him upon gazing at the crown that God had given him. Angels represent natural energies like fire, hail, wind, lighting, whirlwinds, and comets, so knowing the names of the angels and what their names mean gives Enoch power over natural forces. He had transcended and realized God. Then, in an initiation common to mystery schools, Enoch's egoic sense of self is destroyed in a symbolic fire:

> When the Holy One, blessed be he, took me to serve the throne of glory, the wheels of the chariot and all the needs of the Sekinah, at once my flesh turned to flame, my sinews to blazing fire, my bones to juniper coals, my eyelashes to lightning flashes, my eyeballs to fiery torches, the hairs of my head to hot flames, and all my limbs to wings of burning fire, and the substance of my body to blazing fire.

The preceding vision of being purified in a fire represents the destruction of the ego, a common theme in esoteric traditions. The crown represents transcendence in accordance with entering the seventh heaven, another common theme in schools of secret knowledge. The crown represents transcendence over the trammels of the mind and senses, bringing about a state of God realization. These ideas are also addressed in Vedic schools of India, Buddhism in the Himalayas, and the Jewish Kabbalah during the first century. Gentile and Jew—we all come together as one, peace on earth, as it is written.

Then, in 3 Enoch 48A, regarding the Messiah, it is written:

> Then the Holy One, blessed be he, will reveal his great arm in the world, and show it to the gentiles; it shall be as long as the world and as broad as the world, and the glory of its splendor shall be like the brilliant light of the noonday sun at the summer solstice. At once Israel shall be saved from among the gentiles (non Jews) and the Messiah shall appear to them and bring them up to Jerusalem with great joy. Moreover, the kingdom of Israel, gathered from the four quarters of the world, shall eat with the Messiah and the gentiles shall it be with them, as it is written.

The Axial Age

The centuries leading up to Christ are generally known as the axial age (800 to 200 BCE), an age characterized by a shift in consciousness taking place throughout the world at the same time. Perceptions of God were evolving from local deities, to singular prevailing deities, to inconceivable formless beings, and super states of consciousness. It was also a time when more people were looking within to find answers and seeking mystical or spiritual experiences to commune with their Creator. A radical awakening of consciousness was bringing forth most of the world's current religious systems, and key teachers were bringing messages of how to realize God or attain a communion with God.

In India, the **Sanatana Dharma** (eternal truths) were being divined by ancient seers called Rishi's and realized by meditator's called yogis. The oldest of these Vedas, the Rig Veda, which in its written form dates back to 1400 BCE, describes ecstatic experiences while making union with God. During the axial age a collection of Hindu writings called the Upanishads were being developed; they addressed the nature of our existence, the nature of our self and the nature of God. The Hindu concept of god was evolving into something bigger than a man in heaven trying to direct and teach man into a universal intelligence we were all a part of and never separate from. Making this union with God was, and is, the goal of the yogi, and this concept began to be embraced by other cultures...including the first Christians.

The yogis had learned to realize their true divine nature by stilling their mind and turning their awareness inward. Through inner contemplation and meditation, the yogis attained a state of God realization and entered a communion with the divine here on earth that was blissful. These God realized yogis (maharishis, maharajs, and avatars) taught the eternal nature of our own true self. In this theology, our bodies are corruptible and merely vehicles for our spirit (atman); and our purpose in life is to evolve our consciousness to the realization of our true nature. In so doing we would fulfill our life purpose and find enduring happiness and peace. The yogi sought God realization and believed that one day all people would be enlightened, creating paradise on earth. These basic beliefs are also echoed in the teachings of Buddhism which was also born and flourished during the axial age.

What most people who haven't studied Eastern Philosophy don't realize is that such ideas as "the kingdom of god, or heaven, lies within" is a principal tenant of Vedic philosophy, and the realization that "we and are father are one" is the very goal of the Yogi. Christ's metaphor of the blind leading the blind (Matthew 15:14 and Luke 6:39) come right out of Hindu spiritual texts that were written centuries earlier and were widely known in the first century. For instance, in the Mundaka Upanisad (I-ii-8) it states (in the context of man being ignorant of god): "the fools, while being buffeted very much, ramble about like the blind led by the blind alone." Christ's famous metaphor of the mustard seed (Matthew 13:31-32; Mark 4:31-32; Luke 13:18-19) was originally used in the Chandogya Upanishad (3-14-3), centuries earlier in the same context of finding the Divine within the infinitely small. What Christ is teaching is Eastern philosophy, but that should not surprise us since his forefathers were from the East.

In Persia the monotheistic religion of Zoroastrianism developed a new hero called **Mithra**. Mithra is the protector of truth and justice, the source of light and wisdom, the dispeller of ignorance and evil, and a savior of humanity. This god-man was created by God to aid in the destruction of evil on earth and lead people to the righteous path. Over time Mithra becomes a deity and was seen as omniscient and infallible, an incarnation of goodness. Mithra was the messenger of God, and holds a prominent place in world history, for these ideas of an avatar or a god-man had not been a part of Judaism but were entering the consciousness of Judaism through the Persians, Romans, and Greeks who revered him.

During the axial age people were turning to philosophy for hope and understanding. Late in antiquity people worshiped gods and asked the gods for help in a crisis. They sought divine blessings through the priests and found comfort in the establishment of a religious tradition to give them hope, support, and understanding. Religion was based on emotional needs and relied on rituals and rites to give believers a sense of connection with the Creator. During the axial age people started thinking, reflecting, and questioning more, and we see the development of some of the world's great spiritual philosophies. Nowhere is this better reflected than with the Greeks.

In 332 BCE **Alexander the Great** defeated Darius III of Persia, and the Greeks began to colonize Africa and Asia, so the entire Jewish culture was surrounded by Greek rationalism. **Pythagoras**, the sixth-century philosopher and mathematician, believed that the soul was incarcerated in the body, and our true nature was not of this world. There was a higher self, a more evolved or divine aspect of our nature that was eternal and transcendental. **Plato** (428–348 BCE) rejected worship in temples and saw the divine as an unchanging reality beyond the world of the mind and senses. He believed that the soul had fallen from a higher awareness that could be attained again through purification and development of the mind through an inner realization or gnosis.

Through gnosis one could discover the nature of reality and god from within themselves. In the *Symposium*, Plato describes a love and awareness that can be found or attained within the self through contemplation and self-inquiry. Through an inwardly turned consciousness or *theoria* in Greek, one evolves one's consciousness and enters ecstatic realizations and self-awareness. There was something beyond the intellect, the rational, and reason, there was an intuitive understanding of the eternal reality that lies within us. God was a transcendental reality realized through self-inquiry.

Aristotle (384–322 BCE) took this thinking a step further saying that man is a microcosm of the whole universe and to understand God, we must look within ourselves. In Karen Armstrong's *A History of God*, she describes Aristotle's view of the divine: "God was pure being and, as such, eternal, immobile and spiritual. God was pure thought, at one and the same time thinker and thought, engaged in an eternal moment of contemplation of Himself, the highest object of knowledge."

Greek thought and culture in Israel was met with both open arms and contention: those welcoming hellenization were called the **Seleucids** and those opposing it, the **Ptolemics**. When the High Priest Simon II died in 175 BCE, conflict broke out between the supporters of his son Onias III, who opposed hellenization and supported the Ptolemics, and his other son Jason, who favored hellenization and favored the Seleucids. The result was a brief civil war and in 167 BCE the Seleucid king Antiochus IV invaded Judea, stole its possessions, and tried to force the Jews to abandon their laws and customs and embrace hellenization.

This invasion led the Hasmonian priests Mattathias and his sons, including Judah Maccabee, to assume leadership of the famous revolt of the **Maccabees**. Judah Maccabee liberated Jerusalem in 165 BCE and restored the temple and established the Hasmonean Dynasty. The celebration of this victory is called Hanukkah. During this phase the Jews struggled to keep their identity, customs, and beliefs.

The Greeks had also heavily influenced the Egyptian culture and fostered various mystery schools and traditions. The **Therapeutae** were a group of ascetics living in the desert near Alexandria (Egypt) that were considered pious philosophers and healers. Philo described the Therapeutae early in the first century in his book *De vita Contemlativa* (On the Contemplative Life) as being given to "perfect goodness." They were the sages of their time believed to have an ancient and secret wisdom learned through contemplation and meditation.

The Greek Magical Papyri, which in its earliest forms dates back to the second century BCE, casts light on the magico-religious world of Greco-Roman Egypt and gives insights as to what kinds of magical spells were being used by the pagans in those ancient days. These scrolls, written in Greek, are a repository of arcane knowledge, spells, and mystical secrets that were applied by the magicians and faith healers who were common throughout the holy land during this age. Most of the spells refer to a hybrid of Greek and Egyptian gods and goddesses, but by the first century, magicians were also invoking Christ to help drive out demons.

An example of an exorcism spell is as follows: "Speaking over his head; place olive branches before him, and stand behind him and while whipping him with one of the olive branches say" (PGM IV. 1227-64):

> Hail, God of Abraham; hail, God of Isaac, hail God of Jacob; Jesus Chrestos, the Holy Spirit, Son of the Father, who is above the Seven, who is within the seven. Bring Iao Sabaoth, may your power issue forth from him until you drive away this unclean demon Satan, who is in him.

Hermes Trismegistus (thrice-great Hermes) was another god-man who supposedly lived during the time of Moses but was popular in the first century; he had the attributes of both the Greek god Hermes and the Egyptian god Thoth. Thus, the Greek god of communication and revelation was combined with the Egyptian god of wisdom and patron of astrology and alchemy to create a singular deity. Hermitic philosophy rationalized and systematized religious cult practices and offered the adept a method of personal ascension from the constraints of physical being and also developed the pseudoscience of alchemy.

In the first century, Israel lay in the middle of the known civilized world between Asia and Europe and between Asia Minor and Africa. Travel and trade had expanded under the Greeks and then the Romans, and people and information about their cultures were crossing back and forth and through Israel, even as Judaism was redefining its theology and identity. Moreover, Judaism was also influencing the Greco-Roman world. During the first century, approximately one-tenth of the whole empire was Jewish and nearly 40 percent of the population in Alexandria was Jewish. The Jewish concept of one supreme God and a book that dated back into antiquity drew many curious pagans. There were large groups of pagans attending synagogue but not wanting to become circumcised that were known as Godfearers. Judaism was also looking deeper, and a mystical theology was developed that greatly influenced the first-century Christians; that theology was called Kabbalah.

The Kabbalah

Kabbalah (Cabala) means receiving, as in to receive insight from God and represents the mystical aspects of Judaism. It provides an esoteric approach to understanding the Torah or Bible. The purpose of the Kabbalah is to reveal the inner meaning of the stories in the Old Testament such as the meaning of the Tree of Life and the Tree of Knowledge, the name of God (YHWH), as well as to provide insight into the nature of our self and the purpose of our existence. The Kabbalah also provides a greater understanding of the concept of the Messiah and judgment day. Most of its teachings come to us through the Sefer Yetzirah, (Book of Creation), the Bahir (Book of Brightness), while the corpus of literature is known as the Zohar (Book of Splendor).

It is believed that the deeper, secret understanding of the Kabbalah was passed down as an oral tradition from Adam through Noah to Abraham and Moses to the present day, but the written copies don't show up until the Middle Ages. The Kabbalah appears to have been very alive just before and during the time of Christ. In the first century Rabbi Yehoshua, a disciple of Rabbi Yochanan ben Zakaai (47 BCE–73 CE) states he used the Sefer Yetzirah. This does not appear in the Jerusalem Talmud but comes only from other manuscripts from this period. During Christ's time these teachings were passed down to Rabbi Menachem, who Josephus mentions in his Antiquities of the Jews as being an Essene. Thus we have a tie between the Kabbalah and the Essenes, and from the Essenes to Jesus Christ and the early Jewish Christians.

The earliest commentaries of the Kabbalah date back to 931 CE by Saadia Gaon. Rabbi Moshe de Leon (1238–1305 CE) is believed to have published the first copy of the Zohar. A short version called the Mantua was printed in 1562, and in 1550 Rabbi Moshe Cordevero, of the Safed School, developed the Zohar, with the final version attributed to Rabbi Yitzchak Luria, known as the Ari. However, the first English versions of these works only appear in the last few decades.

These teachings have been kept secret for thousands of years and are only now appearing because many Kabbalists believe that the age has come where the people of the world have evolved their awareness to the point that they are ready to receive it. In other words we've entered the age of the Messiah, the age of enlightenment.

Opinions about the Kabbalah and translations of the Zohar vary considerably between Kabalistic schools, and the true and deeper meaning of these teachings doesn't come through information or intellect but through an inner journey invoked through meditation and contemplation of the Torah (Gnosis). Moreover, the Hebrew language is believed to have a power that when the sacred names are enunciated properly, they have the effect of taking the aspirant to higher levels of consciousness, much like mantras in the Sanskrit language of the yogis of India.

The Sefer Yetzirah (Book of Creation) is the oldest of the Kabalistic texts and teaching, and it focuses on God's creation of the universe. Creation is explained in the Sefirot as the Tree of Life. The premise of the teaching is that from the infinite, undifferentiated, potentiality that is God's light the universe was created by removing the light, like "hollowing out a pumpkin," as the light was too much for us to see in its totality. In the Kabbalah, we are told that our own true nature is but a "spark of divinity" rooted in ignorance of our true nature, and life is the process of allowing more light to shine through us through self-reflection and direct awareness.

Yahweh's light comes into the universe like a rainbow of colors from one white light into what are referred to as the ten emanations or Sefirot, and these points of light guide us to attain enlightenment. These ten points of light are arranged in a way that indicates the direction one's spiritual journey must go to attain union with God, and the lessons one must go through as one ascends through the seven levels to enlightenment. Consciousness is rooted or grounded in Malchut, the physically manifest world, and from there ascends through these seven levels of consciousness to Keter or crown, which represents transcendence and the enlightenment of consciousness—God realization. In other words, it's Jewish yoga.

The intension of the aspirant is to transcend differentiation and attain a realization of the interconnected wholeness of creation. In his translation of Sefer Yetzirah (1:8) Aryeh Kaplan quotes:

> **Ten Sefirot of Nothingness**
> **bridle your mouth from speaking**
> **and your heart from thinking**
> **and if your heart runs**
> **return to the place,**
> **it is therefore written,**
> **"The Chayot running and returning" (Ezekiel 1:24)**
> **Regarding this a covenant was made.**

Kaplan further explains this to mean "Only when one makes the mind completely blank can the Sefirot be experienced." Through meditation one realizes the truth. The Kabbalah offers several techniques for attaining these higher states such as the repetition of sacred sounds, contemplation of key phrases or words of the Torah and sitting in stillness. However, the experience only comes after one stops using the techniques and all thought processes are hushed—that is meditation. Through this inner connection one enters chakhmah consciousness and experiences the profound love and awe of God's grace.

The Bahir, or Book of Brightness, is one of the oldest and most important of all classical Kabbalah texts. Attributed to the first century rabbinic sage Nehunya a Ben Ha-Kanah, or by other accounts, to R. Nehunya, a rabbi of the Mishnaic era who lived around 100 CE, the Bahir was first published in the twelfth century in southern France. One of the most important concepts of the Bahir is tzimtzum, the "self-constriction of God's Light." The Ari of the Safed school of Kabbalah explains the Tree of Life (Etz Chaim) as follows:

> Before all things were created...the Supernal Light was simple, and it filled all Existence. There was no empty space...When His simple Will decided to create all universes...He constricted the Light to the sides...leaving a vacated space...This space was perfectly round. After this constriction took place...there was a place in which all things could be created...He then drew a single straight thread from the Infinite Light...and brought it into that vacated space...It was through that line that the Infinite Light was brought down below...

The Zohar gives us a deeper understanding of the stories told in the Torah. Rabbi Philip S. Berg, in his modern English translation of the Zohar explains that the purpose of the Zohar is to "raise our consciousness to a new level" and that "Today we are witnessing the beginning of a new age of revelation." Moreover, the Zohar is transcendental:

> Zohar, our Holy Grail, leads us to a state of mind in which we are connected with the Infinite continuum, where time, space, motion are unified, where past, present and future are entwined, where everyone and everything is interconnected, where then is now, and now is beautiful.

In the Zohar, Beresheet (A, 2), it is written:

> When God created the world, He knew that we, the vessels, could not receive His awesome, blazing Light in its totality. This light is revealed in measure with direct proportion to the degree of change we've undergone, allowing us to receive a greater portion of hidden light.

Therefore, the driving force in the universe comprises the desire for man to make union between the upper world, known as *Zeir Anpin*, and the lower physical dimension *Nukva Malchut*; in other words, we are here to realize God on earth. We are all innately and instinctively being guided by spirit to transcend and make union with the One, as is the case with yoga and Buddhism as well. We draw light from the upper (spiritual) world and bring it into the physical world. This is achieved by resisting our impulses over self-centered desires and allowing our more divine nature to shine through us like light dispelling the darkness.

Life is perceived as a classroom for spirit. We are given choices through our daily life experiences to see how we will do in various circumstances and situations. We can either follow our mind and egoic sense of self-called the Tree of Knowledge (a descent) or we can follow our own indwelling spirit, the Tree of Life (an ascension); this is how we learn, grow, and evolve to full God realization. Rabbi Berg goes on to explain that "obstacles surface to test our commitment and shed light on our negative qualities, so we can confront them and draw from the light." Each time we make the right choice, we ascend in consciousness and get closer to the light. Hell is in our head; it is the absence of God's light. The evil inclination is overcome by sacrificing our ego and surrendering our negative traits, and the state of heaven is realized when we live on earth in the realization of God's living presence within us and around us in everything, everywhere, all the time.

Each day affords us opportunities to fulfill our personal spiritual mission, and it behooves a man or woman to awaken to the spiritual truth of his or her existence, so he or she may develop spiritually and fulfill his or her life purpose. In the Zohar, Vayechi, 49 it is written:

> **The negative angel (force) and the trappings of our seductive material world cause forgetfulness. We succumb to the temptations that glorify our ego, and thus, break our commitment to the Creator.**

According to Rabbi Berg:

> The Kabbalist teach us that the ultimate purpose of life is to evolve our awareness and consequently a deep hatred towards our errant and self-indulgent ways. When our realization and revelation is far greater than our love for selfish pleasure, then God himself will enter our hearts and our very being will destroy every trace of negativity and selfishness that taints our soul. The first and most important precept is to know God, and the principal practice is loving they neighbor as thyself.

The Kabbalah teaches selfless service and unconditional love, which is at the heart of what Jesus Christ taught. The Kabbalah also teaches that the kingdom lies within.

Our Fall from Grace and The Messiah

The metaphor of Adam and Eve and man's fall from grace in the Garden of Eden takes on a new light in the Kabalistic tradition. The Tree of Knowledge represents man's ego, and when relying on his ego, man completely ignores God's rule and denies his loving guidance. God never shunned man; God is all loving, but man shunned God and as a result, he denies himself God's loving divine presence in his life. Heaven is still here on earth, but our eyes are blinded through our self-centered desires and limited thinking. In his introduction to the Zohar, Daniel Matt writes, "The original sin lies in losing intimacy with the Divine, thereby constricting unbounded awareness." When man becomes unaware of God's presence in his life, he suffers. Hell is where our mind goes when not guided by God; in other words, when we go unconscious.

To know God is to know yourself. In the Kabbalah, we are instructed to surrender our egoic nature to realize our true nature as "sparks of divinity" and to serve God by spreading our light until everyone can see.

When the collective light is bright enough, we will all be able to see God's presence within us and around us, in everything, everywhere all the time, and we will have created, or awakened to, the kingdom of heaven on earth. God never left, we have simply been living in ignorance of God's loving presence, and that's why we suffer.

In the Kabbalah, God is not a concept or entity per se but a living presence that is omnipresent, and we are either conscious of it or not. To the degree we are conscious of this consciousness, we ascend in God consciousness, and to the degree that we go unconscious (follow the evil inclination) we suffer. Consciousness is the sense of *I am*. That which is conscious of itself is the consciousness, and it exists within us all. In the Zohar, *Shemot* (8:13) it is written:

> **The first word of the Torah when it was given on Mount Sinai as 'Anochi (I Am)' which is the secret of the first precept of knowing Him.**

In the Kabbalah, it is believed that Hebrew letters each have a special meaning, and by analyzing the meaning of these letters you can gain greater insight into the meaning of a passage, than if you just read the words. This method of decoding the hidden meaning is called **Gematria**. God's name Yahweh (**YHWH** or YHVH) begins with Y for *Yud*, which represents Keter, the crown, the state of total consciousness. God's name means *I am that which I am*. The meaning of this name is *I am* the sense of *I am*. The sense of *I am* is the consciousness; thus God is the consciousness itself. This is an eternal truth that is drawn from each of the world's great religions and in esoteric schools. Consciousness underlies everything that we are conscious of, so as we evolve our own consciousness, we become more conscious of that which we innately are and that which God ultimately is (to the extent the mind can conceive God).

During the age of the Messiah all people will know God and will not need to learn wisdom from one another but rather will have awakened this knowledge from within. According to Rabbi Berg (Zohar, Beresheet A, 21) it is written:

> **The Kabbalists teach that the Messiah is not someone we passively await. Rather, the word Messiah refers to our own individual spiritual actions that will hasten his arrival. Through spiritual growth, we must achieve aspects of the Messiah within ourselves in order to accelerate the arrival of the global Messiah.**

Thus, those who undertake the labor of self-transformation will find themselves living in the light, and those who persist on the path of narcissism will dwell in darkness and discontent. The Messiah represents a state of consciousness in which we are delivered from our egotistical ways and are brought into the light by the word of God. Thus, the Messiah is not thought of as a man, but a revelation of mankind collectively; a time when the collective consciousness of the world awakens to the realization that God never left and that the kingdom of heaven is (and has always been) right here on earth. We have only to open our eyes to see—to be enlightened.

According to the Zohar, the final victory over all the forces of chaos will occur during the age of Aquarius, our present age. Rabbi Abraham Azulai, who lived some 400 years ago, taught that the age of Aquarius is now (roughly the beginning of the new millennium). The age of enlightenment, the age of the Messiah, is upon us. That is why the Zohar has been translated into English for the first time and increasing numbers are interested in reading it; it's getting lots of press. Rabbi Berg tells us:

> **In our day, the intensity of spiritual light is at its highest level in history.**

We have come to the point in the evolution of our consciousness, that we are now consciously seeking ways to further evolve our own consciousness. Once we realize that there is something to be realized, our realization has begun. Having reflected on this, your own consciousness is also awakening—as predicted. As individuals are enlightened, the world is enlightened. As the Bible says *The Kingdom of God is within you* (Luke 17:21). As we collectively awaken our higher consciousness from within, we begin to bring more light into this world, and we create heaven on earth; peace reigns, and the prophesy is fulfilled. Now Jesus shows us how.

. . .

Jeshua ben Joseph the Christ

Jesus Christ was born in Bethlehem, which is in current Palestine. His birth, approximately two thousand years ago, marks the beginning of the common era of recorded history. Born with the Hebrew name *Jeshua ben Joseph* or in Aramaic *Eshoa bar Yosep* (Jesus son of Joseph), or *Y'shua Ha Moshiakh* (Jesus the Messiah), he was born and raised a devout Jew and observed the sacrifices, festivals, and rites of his people and their religion. We also know he was amongst a large body of Jews who questioned the governance of the Jewish temple priests and he was promoting reforms within his religion. It was a time of transition, for the Jews were in the midst of a populist reform movement, similar to the Protestant reformation.

Israel lies at the crossroads of Europe and the East, as well as Africa and Asia Minor. As a result there was strong cross fertilization of cultures and spiritual beliefs in the first century. It was a time when faith healers abounded, and Jewish messiahs, Hermetic sages, and pagan adepts were performing miracles. Talmudic references to tales of faith healers, adepts, and other messiahs in Judaism are plentiful. The Mishnah Ta'anit (3:8) tells the story of Honi the circle drawer who was famous for his ability to successfully pray for rain. One incidence relates that only a drizzle came in response to Honi's prayers for rain. So Honi went back and asked God for more and it began to pour. The

Mishnah Berakot (5:5) recounts the story of how Hanina ben Dosa healed Gamaliel's son through prayer and faith; faith healing and stories of miracles were common and an integral part of the culture at the time. David and other Israelite kings were considered messiah's too. The Jews had a long tradition of kings that freed and united their people and many Jews were expecting yet another.

In 63 BCE the Roman general Pompey captured Jerusalem and inaugurated the period of Roman domination. Pompey ended the monarchy in Israel and named Hyrcanus high priest and ethnarch (a title of leadership lower than king); later, the proconsul of Syria, Antipater, and his sons Phasael and Herod were put in charge. At the time of Christ's ministry, Herod attained the support of Mark Antony and Emperor Octavian in Rome to retain his position as king of the Jews (which officially ended the Hasmonean Dynasty), in return for cooperation with Rome. This made Herod reviled and not trusted by the Jews. Rome placed governors called prefects to rule over their conquered dominion. During the time of Christ the first prefect was Coponius (6–9 CE) and during his ministry, Pontius Pilate (26–36 CE). Annas was high priest of the temple in Jerusalem from 6–15 CE, and his son-in-law Caiaphas from 18–36 CE. Jesus is commonly believed to have preached around 29–36 CE.

Jews were subjugated and were looking for salvation from their plight. Their primary interest was living in peace in Israel, rather than the anticipation of an incarnation of God, an eternal afterlife, or a spiritual awakening. The English word "messiah" comes from the Hebrew word *mashiyakh* or *moshiach* meaning anointed one. King David was considered to be an anointed one. What this word has come to mean to Gentile believers today is very different than its original meaning. Judaism had no prophesy of a God-man, or any need for redemption from original sin. In Judaism there is no original sin from which mankind needs to be saved. The understanding from the Old Testament is that there is evil, mankind is tested, and regularly disobeys God's laws and sins, but this has not tainted mankind forever. The concept of original sin and redemption comes from within the pagan culture and will be discussed in later chapters. The Messiah the Jews were hoping for was a Davidic king or a man like Moses, who would lead their people to glory and establish the state of Israel, free from foreign domination, where they could live in peace with God—the fulfillment of God's promise to Abraham. This is why the Jews never accepted Jesus as their Messiah, they have had no peace until now.

As discussed in the preceding chapter, during the time of Christ, the Kabbalah was entering into a golden age and a deeper meaning and understanding of biblical stories were beginning to be disseminated. The Bible's stories were understood to be metaphorical, not literal, conveying messages that would help us understand God's will. Moreover, after Alexander the Great (356–323 BCE) conquered the whole region, all of Israel fell under the influence of the Greek culture, in other words it became Hellenized. Plato, Socrates, Aristotle, the Epicureans, and Stoics were all influencing this new emerging culture and religion. Plato's concept of gnosis, an awaking of consciousness or inner knowing, was introduced at the same time that the Kabalistic concept of enlightenment was developed. It was a spiritual renaissance, the beginning of the Piscean age.

Jesus lived and ministered primarily in northern Israel, in the communities of Nazareth and Galilee. He preached primarily to the poor. His father, Joseph, was a tradesman, and Jesus, along with his brothers and sisters, likely worked as carpenters and masons building the new Roman cites in the region. The first followers of Christ were Jews. We know some members of his family would follow him (his mother Mary and brother James), as would local fishermen (Peter and Andrew) and businessmen (Matthew). He appealed to the poor and disenfranchised, sometimes called *Ebionites*. Some of the earliest Christians were the Hebrews, Syrians, and Egyptians. Some of the first followers of Jesus include the Essene sects, followers of John the Baptist, and a group of gentiles (non-Jews) called God fearers, who were drawn to Judaism. The Aramaic speaking people of Syria and Mesopotamia were also among the first to start churches, record, and follow Christ's teachings. The Greek and Romans converts came several years later and will be discussed at great length in succeeding chapters.

The Aramaic Gospels

Jesus spoke in the ancient Syriac language of **Aramaic** (*Leshana Aramaya*), a sister language of Hebrew that was spoken throughout Syria, Mesopotamia, as well as Palestine and Israel, in the first century. Jesus' first followers spoke Aramaic, and it was the language used in the first churches, and the language that first recorded the life and teachings of Jesus. Thus, Aramaic provides the most accurate account and meaning of the words that Jesus spoke. The **Peshitta** is the authorized Bible in its original language, dating to the early part of the second century. It is this Aramaic Bible that has been used by the people of Palestine, Syria, Mount Lebanon, Mesopotamia, Persia, and the Malabar Coast of India from the first century to today. It's still a living language in isolated parts of the world, and the Peshitta is still being used.

According to Dr. George M. Lamsa, one of the world's leading scholars of the Aramaic language and translator of the Peshitta to English:

> Peshitta is still the text of more than a million Maronites, Chaldean Roman Catholics in the Near East, the Jacobites, the Malkites and Assyrian Christians. These people are the remnant of the ancient churches of Galilee, Jerusalem, Damascus, Antioch and Edessa. Both the Peshitta *Old* and New Testaments were also used by the Armenians until the fifth century when a translation into the Armenian language was made.

Even before Paul's conversion, the Aramaic-speaking Semites began spreading the good news in Syria, Mesopotamia, Persia, and India. The Persian kings accepted these Jewish-Christians, but because of repeated wars with the Romans, the Eastern churches became estranged from the newer Greek Orthodox or Roman Catholic Churches that were under Roman domination. These Eastern churches continued speaking and reading in Jesus' mother tongue and continue to read from the original writing of the New Testament which, according to Dr. Lamsa, differs considerably from the Greek translations. Matter of fact, the Eastern (Aramaic) churches rejected the Greek translations and the councils of the Greco-Roman churches, and stuck with the original Christian scriptures and their original meaning, practices, and beliefs.

With the rise of Islam in the sixth century, the Near East Christians were lost to the rest of Christendom along with the Peshitta, but they continued in isolated communities, such as northern Iraq, for thousands of years, practicing Christianity as Semitic Christians practiced it in the first century. Dr. Lamsa writes in his book *The Modern New Testament from the Aramaic* that "this isolation continued through Arab, Mongol and Turkish rule from the sixth to the thirteenth century. As the result of this continued isolation, the biblical customs and manners and Aramaic language remained unchanged and the **Scriptures escaped additions and revisions**." When Mesopotamia was opened to the West by the British after the first World War, these Eastern churches and their writings became known to biblical scholars, but they are only now beginning to enter the public domain and they are giving us greater insight into the original meaning of Jesus' life and teachings.

Semite Christians never used the *Greek* Septuagint Bible and the Eastern church still does not because they have the original gospels from which the Greek was translated; moreover, they believe the Greek translations (including the later Latin and English versions) are full of revisions, mistranslations, and errors. In the Aramaic version of the Gospel of Matthew, for instance, **the last chapters describing Christ's ascension are not included**. The ascension story is not included in the Gospel of Mark either. The Greco-Roman churches added the ascension stories sometime in the early second century. The ascension was not a part of Semite Christian belief; it comes from the Greek interpretation within their pagan paradigm of heaven and hell. These Semite Christians who were closest to Jesus did not believe that Jesus was born of a virgin; they believed that he was Joseph's natural son. Nor did they believe that Jesus was a god but, rather, that he was the Messiah who was going to deliver them from oppression. According to Rocco A. Errico and George M. Lamsa in their *Aramaic Light on the Gospel of Matthew*:

> **These early Church Fathers said that Mary was the mother of Jesus and was not the mother of God. They also taught that Jesus died on the cross as a man.**

According to the Semite Christian rendering of Christ's teachings, "Jesus revealed to humanity a loving all-inclusive presence he called Father." Jesus was known to meditate at the edge of the desert and that he taught that the "Kingdom was at hand" here and now; they believed that Jesus was showing us the way to realize this kingdom here on earth. The presence of God was at hand, and Jesus was showing us the way to realize this living presence of the Father here on earth, which is enlightenment. In his book *Setting a Trap for God*, Errico further explains this Near Eastern perspective of Abba—the Father—as an infinite intelligence that is guiding us from within: "Spiritual powers have always been within the hearts and souls of all human beings. But we often look for something that is outside of ourselves, not fully realizing that we are God's image and likeness." The path to God was to seek him within, and Jesus was showing us the way to enlightenment while he walked on this earth. We become enlightened through his word, we become *Christ enlightened*.

Jewish Christians

Although the world's biblical scholars know about the beliefs and practices of these first century Jewish Christians, and this information is published and even appears in best-selling books, most clergy avoid discussions on the matter and dismiss these writings out of hand. These ideas are so different from what we think of as Christianity today that they are difficult for a Christian to even conceive of, let alone believe. Fortunately we have well-documented records of what these first followers of Jesus believed and practiced. Matter of fact, this new information about these earliest followers of Christ predates New Testament gospels; all the gospels started as oral traditions and the first oral traditions were started by those Jewish Christians who actually walked with Jesus, spoke Aramaic, and lived in Israel. The lost gospels.

In the past few decades so many codexes (books made from papyrus), dating back to the first and second centuries (as well as third and fourth), have been excavated from archeological sites in Egypt, Israel, Palestine, Jordan, and Syria that a whole new understanding of Christ's teachings is developing. Some of the earliest gospels ever written had been lost or languishing in obscurity until recently. These include the Gospel of the Ebionites, the Gospel of the Nazereans, the Gospel of the Hebrews, the Gospel of the Egyptians, the Dialog with the Savior, and The Thunder Perfect Mind, as well as many others. (*The Gospels of Thomas, James, Philip, and Mary will be discussed in the next chapter.*)

From the **Nag Hammadi library**, which was discovered in 1945, in ancient urns buried in the desert sands of Nag Hammadi, Egypt, we gained a wealth of information about these first Christians. According to James M. Robinson, general Editor of the Nag Hammadi Library, and professor emeritus of Religion a Claremont Graduate University:

> **Those who collected this library were Christians, and many of the essays were originally composed by Christian authors.**

According to Robinson, summarizing what is in this collection of books (Introduction):

> **Jesus called for a full reversal of values, advocating the end of the world as we have known it and its replacement by a quite new, utopian kind of life in which the ideal would be real. He took a stand quite independent of the authorities of his day…and did not last long before they eliminated him. Yet his followers reaffirmed his stand - for them he came to personify the ultimate goal.**

Many of these books we have already heard about from references of the church fathers of the third and fourth centuries. We've had scraps of some of these books sitting in various museums and universities around the world (e.g., the Berlin Codex), and we know that they were in popular use in the first century, but we previously didn't know much about them. But over the last fifty years more Christian scripture has been discovered than exists in the entire New Testament. The experts in the field have scrutinized these codexes for over four decades now, and the consensus is that these documents are authentic and were used by Christians in the first and second centuries. That means the very first Christians, the ones who actually walked with Jesus and his disciples, and their children and grandchildren, are the ones who first told these stories and wrote them down and are the ones that used these documents (which I will discuss here). This information paints a whole new picture of early Christianity, as you will see.

One of the first points of interest is that the followers of Jesus never actually called themselves Christians but referred to Christ's teachings as *the way* (Luke 9:59, 24:35, Mark 10:52, John 14:6, Acts 18:26). They were Jews who observed the traditional Jewish holidays, Mosaic, and dietary laws and required circumcision. Second, they saw Jesus as the new king from the lineage of King David and believed he was the natural born son of Mary and Joseph. They believed he was going to deliver them from Roman bondage and create the state of Israel that had been promised and prophesized.

In Judaism there was no and is no mythology of a virgin birth or Immaculate Conception. The references cited in the New Testament that the Old Testament suggest the Messiah would be **born of a virgin** *(Isaiah 7:14)* are incorrect, the word actually used means *young woman* (of child bearing age) not a virgin. Jews have never expected their Messiah to be born of a virgin or to have an immaculate conception. Yet, very few Christians realize this. Virgin births were a part of the Greco-Roman culture, particularly Mithran cults, which we will explore later. The Greek god Zeus would have divine copulation with humans and give birth to divine human beings, but this was completely foreign to Jewish culture and tradition. For Jesus to be the Messiah, he was expected to be of the bloodline of Joseph, his father, just like kings of other nations (he's *ben Joseph*—son of Joseph). Moreover, many of these early followers knew Jesus and his family personally, and they knew better. The Greco-Roman church fathers of the second and third centuries were very disturbed that the Jewish Christians from the Holy Land and the Eastern churches never accepted Jesus' Immaculate Conception.

Another shocking realization about the first followers of Christ is that they did not believe that Jesus died on the cross for the remission of their sins and neither did the other Semite Christians in Syria, Persia, or India; none of the children or grandchildren of the original disciples from Israel believed that Jesus died for remission of their sin. This was a completely foreign concept to first century Jews who had no precedent for anyone dying in remission for their sins, and they already had protocols for penance. According to historians, the first Christians saw Jesus as a martyr, a self-sacrificing man who was showing them the way to the kingdom of heaven on earth as their messianic leader. They called him rabbi, teacher, or master, and their salvation was finding their peace from within. He was never considered a deity, and he did not die for our sins but died trying to show us how not to sin. The kingdom of heaven was not going to come some day in the future; it was dawning. Heaven was being realized through Jesus by following him and hearing his word. He was showing the way to salvation from the hell on earth by finding heaven within through him while he was still alive. He was enlightening them.

Jesus teaches *the way*

The first followers of Christ referred to their path to enlightenment as "the way." They were seeking enlightenment; they were searching for peace, knowledge, and communion with God. Jesus shows us the way to enlightenment by going within and coming to our own realization as to our own true nature and purpose. Long before Saint Paul converted to Christianity, these first followers of Jesus had formed congregations of their own. Jesus had made James head of the church, and this first generation of Christians were practicing a form of Christianity much different from what we recognize today. Moreover, when Paul began preaching years later, his teachings were rejected by these first followers of Jesus.

The New Testament book of Acts (15) cites a meeting in which the apostles agreed that gentiles did not need to be circumcised or adhere to dietary laws, but according to historians, the Jewish followers rejected these ideas and resented Paul for minimizing Mosaic laws. Paul never actually met or studied with Jesus while he walked on this earth and, according to the book of Acts, Paul developed a reputation for killing Christians prior to converting, so it's understandable that those earliest disciples questioned Paul's authority to teach or dictate new laws. As shocking as it sounds, they never considered Paul an apostle. The church fathers of the second and third centuries make this clear in their letters. The Christians in the Holy Land, those that walked with Jesus, rejected Paul's writings, and his disciples never accepted the pagan paradigms of Christ that came from within the Greco-Roman culture. They thought what Paul taught was objectionable and quite different from what they thought Christ was teaching.

The earliest followers of Christ of whom we are aware include the Ebionites, the Nazareans, the Hebrews, and the Egyptians, and each group has its own gospel. Most of what we know about these groups we obtain from what the church fathers of the late second and third centuries discussed in their correspondence or in essays. The following gospels help clarify what Christianity was really like in the first century.

The Gospel of the Ebionites

The Gospel of the Ebionites, from the late first century, comes to us from the very first Jewish followers of Jesus who believed he was the

Messiah who would lead them to freedom and peace in Israel. Ebionite comes from the Hebrew word *Ebyonim*, which means the Poor Ones since Christ's first followers were from the lower working classes who were most afflicted by the political, military, and economic conditions of the age. They existed from the first to fourth centuries until first the Romans and later the orthodox church eliminated them. There was an emphasis on the Mosaic law, and they referred to their Hebrew (Aramaic) version of Gospel of Matthew but didn't include any of Paul's writings. They were among the largest sects of Christianity in the first century and among the first to actually study with Christ and the apostles directly. Ebionites did not believe in an immaculate conception, the resurrection, or that Jesus died for the remission of our sin. They thought Jesus was the Jewish Messiah who had come to show them *the way*. In Bart D. Ehrman's book *Lost Scriptures: Books That Did Not Make It into the New Testament* he states:

> **They were said to have emphasized belief in only one God to such an extent that they denied, as a consequence, Jesus' own divinity.**

Almost two centuries later, while the orthodox church was consolidating power and control over the teachings of Jesus, the church father Irenaeus (180 CE) stated that they were a "heretical judaizing sect" that stubbornly clung to the old law. Some Ebionite sects are believed by church fathers to include the Carpocratians, the Cerinthians, the Elcesaites, the Sampsaeans, and possibly the Nazarenes and Nazoraeans, according to church father **Epiphanius**. They celebrated the Passover and the traditional Jewish Sabbath and considered James to be a blood bother of Jesus, and their leader. Many of the Ebionites had been followers of **John the Baptist** and still thought of John as one of the leaders of their movement. It was John's recognition of Jesus that helped the Jesus movement gain a following among the Ebionites.

All we have of this gospel is fragments of what the church fathers had written about them. The following is a quote from the church father Epiphanius, in his *Panarion* (30, 13, 6):

> The beginning of the Gospel they use reads as follows 'And so in the days of Herod, King of Judea, John came baptizing a baptism of repentance in the Jordan River. He was said to have come from the tribe of Aaron, the priest, and was the child of Zacharias and Elizabeth. And everyone went out to him.

In *Panarion* (30, 13, 3-4) Epiphanius gives the familiar description of Jesus receiving a baptism from John and the Holy Spirit descending on him in the form of a dove, and a voice from heaven stating "You are my beloved Son, in you I am well pleased," which is generally believed to be the recognition of Jesus as the Christ and the beginning of his ministry. But then the voice from heaven goes on to say:

> Today I have given you birth. Immediately a great light enlightened the place. When John saw this it says, he said to him, "Who are you Lord?" Yet again a voice came from heaven to him, "This is my beloved Son, with whom I am well pleased."

Similar passages occur in Matthew 3:17 and 17:5, in Mark 1:11 and Luke 3:22. So, apparently, Jesus was enlightened during his baptism with John the Baptist and was recognized by John's followers at this time.

The Gospel of the Nazareans

The Gospel of the Nazareans (Nazarenes), from the first to early second century, comes to us from those who came from Jesus' home of Nazareth in northern Israel. They were among the first groups to follow Jesus. A Nazarite was a Jew who had taken special vows of dedication to the Lord whereby he abstained for a specified period of time from using alcohol and grape products, cutting his hair, and approaching corpses. In the Gospel of Philip, which we return to later, it describes how the word *nazara* means truth and states: "Nazara is the Truth." Therefore *Nazarenos* is the One of the Truth. Epiphanius, in his book *Panarion* 29 states:

> But these sectarians...did not call themselves Christians but "Nazarenes."...They acknowledge both the resurrection of the dead and the divine creation of all things, and declare that God is one, and that his son is Jesus the Christ.

Epiphanius goes on further in the same section to say:

> They disagree with Jews because they have come to faith in Christ; but since they are still fettered by the Law—circumcision, the Sabbath, and the rest— they are not in accord with Christians... they are nothing but Jews...They have the Good News according to Matthew in its entirely in Hebrew."

Interestingly, although the Nazarenes studied the Gospel according to Matthew in Hebrew, their gospel, likely one of the earliest versions (if not the first), it did not record the first two chapters of Jesus' miraculous birth. That was, apparently, written in later when translated to Greek. Nazarenes did not believe Jesus was divine although they believed that he was being divinely guided to guide them. They saw him as their master but not as a god. He died a martyr—not for remission of their sin, but, rather, as a righteous teacher, or rabbi, saving them from the plight they were in . The church father Origen gives us some more details of his understanding of their beliefs in his *Commentary on Matthew* (15, 14) where in the Nazarean Gospel a rich man asks Jesus a question and Jesus replies:

> "Master, what good thing must I do to have life? He replied to him, "O man, you should keep the law and the prophets." He responded, "I have already done that."Jesus said to him, "Go, sell all that you have and distribute the proceeds to the poor; then come follow me."

The followers of Christ were like the followers of gurus in India or the Buddha who renounce money and worldly possessions, and shun the materialistic world. Their teachings focused not on sin, guilt, and shame but, rather, on love and selfless service to others as Jesus exemplified and taught. They were contemplative and were peace activists, shunning the Zealots and their uprisings. Their lifestyle and beliefs were more akin to those of the Essenes, and they kept the Jewish Sabbath and festivals. According to Aramaic scholar Rocco A. Errico in his book *Setting a Trap for God*:

> **Many Bible instructors continue to teach that we must approach God as if we were totally degraded, full of sin, no good, and unworthy human beings. This is not interpreting Scripture correctly! Jesus never taught this!**

The earliest accounts of what Jesus taught and what the disciples practiced involved finding God within and serving your fellow man selflessly. Origen goes on to say in his *Commentary on Matthew* (15, 14) further explaining to the rich man asking Jesus questions:

> **You shall love your neighbor as yourself. But look, many of your brothers, sons of Abraham, are clothed in excrement and dying of hunger while your house is filled with many good things, not one of which goes forth to these others.**

Then, turning to Simon who was sitting beside him, we hear another application of a popular metaphor of Christ's (Mark 10:25, Luke 18:25). According to Origen, quoting the Gospel of the Nazareans, Jesus says, "Simon, son of Jonah, it is easier for a camel to pass through the eye of a needle than for a rich person to enter the kingdom of heaven." Christ's teachings centered on compassion, charity, and forgiveness. There is no evidence of sin and redemption in their teachings, and this is one of the reasons that the Greco-Roman church never accepted their gospels. Moreover, they never accepted the authority of the church in Rome over them, so the bishops of the empire excluded them. Jerome, another church father we will come back to, recounts what Jesus says in the Nazarean gospel, as recorded in his book *Against the Pelagians* (3, 2):

> If your brother sins by speaking a word against you, but then makes it up to you, you should accept him seven times a day.

Then Simon turns to Jesus and says, "Seven times in a day?" And Jesus responds,

> Yes indeed, I tell you—even up to seventy times seven! For even among the prophets, after they were anointed by the Holy Spirit, a word of sin was found.

The Nazareans focused on Jesus' mission as the Messiah and did not include the story of Jesus' miraculous birth. Quoting *Lost Scriptures*, by Bart D. Ehrman, chairman of the Department of Religious Studies at the University of North Carolina at Chapel Hill:

> According to many Jewish Christians, Jesus was not born of a virgin, but was a natural human being who was specially chosen to be the messiah because God considered him to be more righteous than anyone else.

The Gospel According to the Hebrews

The Gospel According to the Hebrews, from the first half of the second century, was another gospel that was well read by the early followers of Christ and was later rejected by the Greco-Roman church. We only have scattered references from church fathers. It supports the importance of James as head of the community in Jerusalem and focuses on Jesus' ethical teachings and on our relationship with the

Holy Spirit. Origen quotes from it in his *Commentary on John* (2, 12), quoting Jesus:

> Just now my mother, the Holy Spirit, took me by one of my hairs and carried me up.

His mother is the Holy Spirit, and what he was teaching was that we are spirit. The word spirit in Hebrew is in the feminine gender and sometimes referred to as the *Shekinah*. This word refers to the energy-consciousness that makes things manifest; that which comes from heaven to manifest on earth via the Shekinah or Holy Spirit. Two important concepts are emphasize (1) the Lord is the Spirit (not the man) and (2) when you realize that divine presence, or spirit, within you there is liberty from the trammels of the mind and senses. We are guided to realize our own divine nature as spirit, what is called the spark of divinity in the Kabbalah. The church father Jerome, in his *Commentary on Isaiah* (11:1-3), quotes from the *Gospel of the Hebrews*, which further explains this, quoting the Hebrew followers of Christ:

> The entire fountain of the Holy Spirit will descend on him. For the Lord is the Spirit, and where the Spirit of the Lord is, there is liberty.

In the Aramaic version of the New Testament, we gain deeper insight as to our divine relationship with God, the Holy Spirit, and Jesus that reflects the Hebrew perspective—we are one in Christ. We are one in spirit, we are one in consciousness, and we are one with God; this is a state of consciousness. We are realizing the living presence of God within us. Dr. Errico interprets the Gospel of John from the Peshitta or Aramaic Bible:

> But you know him (the spirit of Truth) because he dwells with you and is in you (John 14:17). Moreover, in that day you will know that I am in my Father, and you are in me, and I am in you (John 14:20).

The Gospel of the Egyptians

The Gospel of the Egyptians, from the early second century, is believed to have originated with the followers of Jesus in Egypt, which was one of the most receptive areas to Christ's teachings in the first century. Egypt at that time was home to many of the desert fathers who lived like hermits in the deserts of South Israel and in Egypt (the Nagev and Sinai). Several of the church fathers make mention of them, but we learn the most from Clement of Alexandria (Egypt). Again, these followers of Christ also see him as a messiah, as a man not a god, and, again, that salvation comes from within. In Clement of Alexandria's book *Miscellanies* (3, 63, 10), Clement quotes and comments on a passage from the Gospel of the Egyptians in a discussion between Christ and one of his female disciples, Salome:

> **Salome asked, "How long will people continue to die?" and Jesus replies: "For as long as women bear children."**

Clement goes on to say that, that means for as long as we continue to have desires and procreate, we will experience physical death. Jesus explains that we are not our physical bodies, and they can be dropped like an old garment, for we are the eternal spirit. Then again in *Miscellanies* (3, 92, 2-93, 1), he comes back to a question Salome asks regarding when she will attain enlightenment, Jesus is quoted as saying:

> **When you trample on the shameful garment and the two become one and the male with the female is neither male nor female.**

In classical wisdom teachings this refers to the transcendence of the mind and body, and the union of the individual spirit with the Holy Spirit, which, in fact, is one. Our apparent differentiation from God is caused by our self-identification with the temporal physical body, which is the ultimate cause of our suffering. When you realize your true nature, as spirit (consciousness in expression), you join with

Christ in consciousness and realize the true nature of the self, which is neither male nor female. Jesus is teaching the classic, universal approach to God realization—Jesus taught enlightenment.

The Dialogue of the Savior

The Dialogue of the Savior is one of the oldest of the codexes found in Egypt in Nag Hammadi; scholars argue over the exact date of its origin, which was sometime before the end of the first century. Stephen Emmel discovered other fragments of this scripture (144, 15-146, 24) that had been in the Beinecke Library at Yale University, but were only recently identified as being from the Dialogue of the Savior. The speaker is Jesus, and he is explaining to his disciples our true nature and how to find salvation through self-realization. Jesus is teaching the disciples how to come to know themselves, so that they may be liberated and realize God. Many of the sayings are echoed in the New Testament gospels and in the Gospels of Mary and Thomas, which also are among the oldest gospels written. In The Dialogue with the Savior, Mary Magdalena is recognized and receives the highest praise from the Lord, and Thomas, Mary, and Matthew are all given a glimpse of hell, and they all come to realize that the material world is an evil created through men living in ignorance of their own true nature.

After expounding on creation, The Dialogue of the Savior returns to a question and answer session with the disciples on how to achieve salvation through gnosis. This codex is heavily damaged and much of the text is missing, which makes most of it difficult to translate clearly. However, there are a few sections that stand out clearly and give us a much greater understanding of what those first Jewish Christians were thinking. We come to know God by appearing to be separate from God—like standing outside of ourselves to know our self or looking in a mirror to self-reflect. Our true nature is revealed through introspection and self-inquiry. The Dialogue then states in section 34:

"If one does not stand in the darkness, he will not be able to see the light." From darkness, as we turn to behold the light within we see, as explained in verse 53:

> If one does not understand how fire came into existence, he will burn in it, because he does not know the root of it. If one does not first understand water, he knows nothing. For what use is there for him to be baptized in it? If one does not understand how blowing wind came into existence, he will blow away with it. If one does not understand how the body, which he bears came into existence, he will perish with it. And how will someone who does not know the Son know the Father? And to someone who will not know the root of wickedness is no stranger to it. Whoever will not understand how he came will not understand how he will go…

Here we are told of the transient nature of our body, and the eternal nature of our true self and that it is our calling to find ourselves and allow that inner light to shine. Jesus tells us (section 57) "But I say to you that when what invigorates a man is removed, he will be called dead. And when what is alive leaves what is dead, what is alive will be called upon." And then he clarifies (59): "Whatever is born of truth does not die. Whatever is born (of) a woman dies." In other words, we are not our bodies; we are the eternal spirit. Then Judas asks, "Tell me, Lord, what the beginning of the path is?" To which Jesus replies, "Love and goodness." The way is the path of the heart, and you find him, and join him, within. According to Jesus, those who come to *know themselves* come to know God—they attain God realization. Then Jesus explains how to enter the kingdom through self-inquiry (27-30):

> Matthew said "Lord, I want to see that place of light…where there is no wickedness, but rather there is pure light! The Lord said, "Brother Matthew, you will not be able to see it as long as you are carrying flesh around." Matthew said, "Lord, even if I will not be able to see it, let me know it." The Lord said, "Everyone who has known himself has seen it in everything given to him to do."

The Thunder Perfect Mind

The Thunder Perfect Mind comes to us through the Nag Hammadi Library and attempts to explain the transcendent state of consciousness attained by following the way; The Thunder Perfect Mind is an enlightened mind. This codex attempts to explain enlightenment and the nature of existence. It is written as a poem, or affirmation, declaring and/or describing a state of nonduality and recognizing the inner essence of our own being, our very sense of *I am*. Again, these teachings are universal and similar examples referring to this state of I am occur in the Bhagavad-Gita (IX, 16-19), Atharva-Veda (X, viii, 27-28), the Svetasvatara Upanishad (IV, 3), and the Bible in Genesis. It's the root of God's (Yahweh's) very name (YHWH). As discussed earlier, God's name in Hebrew means *I am that which I am* or just *I am*; that which is conscious of itself is the consciousness itself. Early Christians sought to find God within and The Thunder Perfect Mind explains the state that they were seeking under Jesus' guidance.

The Thunder Perfect Mind attempts to describe the state of enlightenment. Thunder is the voice from above, the voice of heaven, the voice of God. Perfect mind, or intellect, refers to the state of total awareness. They were seeking the union of their awareness with the voice of heaven within or the voice of God within or the presence of God within. Later, the church looked down on these views because they involve the follower going within for answers rather than to following a priest, bishop, or pope. This codex explains the experience of gnosis better than the others. To contemplate this scripture is a meditation in itself. The Thunder Perfect Mind begins as follows:

> "[A]nd I have been found among those who seek after me. Look upon me, you (plural) who reflect upon me, and you hearers, hear me. You who are waiting for me, take me to yourselves, and do not banish me from your sight. And do not make your voice hate me, nor your hearing. Do not be ignorant of me anywhere or any time. Be on your guard! Do not be ignorant of me."

God in heaven was seen as the power that created and sustains the universe and that which we merge back into, or join, after death or enlightenment. The emphasis is on self-reflection to gain gnosis and transcend ignorance. This practice, also known as mindfulness, involves being conscious of the divine presence in everything, everywhere, all the time. The goal was to transcend ignorance and come into full knowledge of God—God realization. These concepts are further developed in both the Kabbalah and in Christian Gnosticism. This scripture then dives into the nature of duality and the transcendent:

> For I am the first and the last. I am the honored one and the scorned one. I am the whore and the holy one. I am the wife and the virgin.

This cryptic writing is similar to the classic style of yoga philosophy taught by the Rishis of India called **Jhana Yoga** or Vedanta, something a devotee of Shiva or An would teach. She says, I am the first and the last. Similar to Christ's statement that "I am the Alpha and the Omega" (Rev. 1:8, 1:11, 21:6 and 22:13). The esoteric meaning is that God was before the beginning and after the end and is timeless and transcendent. The contrasts between honored and scorn, whore and holy, wife and virgin denotes that the truth lies beyond judgment, beyond the mind. Our eating from the Tree of Knowledge of Good and Evil created a faculty of judgment—the ego. Our mind creates these differences and polarities whereas God is transcendent to them. Then it goes still further:

> I am the knowledge of my inquiry, and the finding of those who seek after me, and the command of those who ask for me, and the power of powers in my knowledge of the angels, who have been sent at my word, and the gods in their seasons by my counsel, and of spirits of every man who exists with me, and of women who dwell within me.

So God is what is realized when one inquires into the nature of God, and that which is compelling us to seek him *is* him within us. The very volition to seek God is from God. Angels represent the energy that protects and guides us on our path to God realization. God is expressed through the spirit, and this spirit lies within every man and woman; we are all spirit and all connected with him in spirit and through spirit. We are all part of the one, like cells in the body of God. This scripture then goes on to describe our true intrinsic nature:

> For what is inside you is what is outside you, and the one who fashions you on the outside is the one who shaped the inside of you. And what you see outside of you, you see inside of you; it is invisible and it is your garment.

What is inside of you and outside of you is the consciousness itself. The consciousness in expression is the Holy Spirit and that is what animates your and our existence. When you come to know your self, you come to know the essence of existence. We also receive some Kabalistic elements in this scripture, referring to the name of the sound and the sound of the name. In Kabbalah the words have deeper meaning that takes us to a state beyond meaning. In the following verses we receive this inner secret:

> Hear me, you hearers, and learn of my words, you who know me. I am the hearing that is attainable to everything; I am the speech that cannot be grasped. I am the name of the sound and the sound of the name.

So here we go back to the meaning of God's name in Hebrew (Yahweh), which means *I am* or *I am that which I am* or *I am this*. Sometimes this reference is believed to be God being cheeky and not wanting to reveal his name. Reflecting on the name of God and its meaning is the meditation devise used to realize God. This realization of God's name and its meaning also appears in numerous esoteric teachings; it is the path to enlightenment. That which is conscious of the self is the self;

you are the consciousness itself. Knowing the self, in its many renditions, is the path to enlightenment. I am not suggesting that Jesus copied or adopted an Eastern religion, but rather that enlightened masters teach similar teachings, and who is more enlightened than Jesus?

Christ is teaching the universal path to enlightenment. In realizing the true nature of ourselves, we come to realize the true nature of God. When Christ states in John (10:30) "I and my Father are one" this is what he means. He is one in spirit, one in consciousness. He is not bragging; he sharing a universal truth—we are all one in spirit. We are to join him in spirit and be of one consciousness. We all draw our life from the same source, and we are all connected in spirit, as spirit. In other words, we join him in spirit. The kingdom of Heaven is a spiritual kingdom; it is a state of consciousness attained here on earth right now.

. . .

The Apostles' Canon

Most of what we know about the life and teachings of Jesus Christ has come to us from a very select group of documents called the New Testament. In the New Testament we have the four gospels of Matthew, Mark, Luke, which tell very similar accounts of Jesus' life and ministry (called the Synoptic Gospels), and the Gospel of John, which focuses on Jesus' miracles and good works. We also have an accounting of the initial Acts of the Apostles, as well as, letters written by and to apostles and their churches called the epistles. The New Testament ends with an account of a vision of the day of judgment, which is attributed to John, called Revelation. We don't know who wrote any of the gospels, but scholars believe that disciples of the apostles wrote down what they said, including what they said Jesus said, and those writings were further copied, and recopied many times over until we get the oldest known physical copy, which dates to the fourth century.

The final version of this compilation of writing was collected, debated, selected, edited, and finally published around three hundred years after Christ's crucifixion, when Emperor Constantine commissioned the first Bibles to be written in 325 CE (the actual canon came several years later). This selection of writings became known as the churches' Canon, the official orthodox version of the New Testament. Until recently, most people had no idea that there were other gospels or scriptures that Christians in the first and second centuries used. Archeological discoveries in the Middle East over the past few decades have revealed dozens of new Christian texts, many of which we have heard about from the writings of the church fathers, but the contents of which have been lost or destroyed over time. Now we know or at least know more of what those other gospels had to say. Scholars from around the world have been studying and debating the interpretations and contexts of these works and we now have a much clearer understanding of what the first followers of Christ were taught in the first century. This has opened up a whole new understanding of Christ's word.

From the time of Christ's ministry to the formation of the Canon was a span of around 300 years. To put that in perspective, imagine Christ living just 300 years ago; that's over 100 years before the American Revolution. Imagine the changes in history, culture, and the lexicon that occurred over that time span. That's like going back to the time of Isaac Newton and the rise of Peter the Great as tsar of Russia (1680s). Moreover, we have a much better accounting of the history from 300 ago than we do from 2,000 years ago. From the time of Christ's teachings to the consolidation of the Church's canon a gigantic shift in beliefs occurred. These teachings changed, and continue to be revised or reinterpreted, as is demonstrated through the divisions of the Orthodox, Catholic and Protestant religions, and more recently with the new age evangelical movement.

During the first and second centuries there were many different Christian sects. Apostles spread out to neighboring lands to preach the good news, and the churches that formed around them tended to follow the presentation of their particular teacher, who each provided different insights and information to share about what they learned from Jesus. There were actually many gospels in the first and second centuries. Many of the gospels that Christians read in the first 200 years have been lost to the modern world. Over two-thirds of what Jesus was reported to have said and was recorded in the first and second centuries, and studied by Christians for hundreds of years was omitted from the New Testament. Most of what early Christians read and taught in church, and believed for hundreds of years, has been kept from us, until now. First let us introduce the twelve apostles.

The Twelve Apostles

The word *apostle* is Greek (*apostolos*) and means someone sent out (with a message) and more specifically refers to the twelve apostles Christ personally chose to represent him and preach the gospel. Later this term was expanded to include other early evangelists who had not actually been chosen by Jesus but served as missionaries on his behalf, including Paul, Barnabus, or Matthias, and still later, Saint Patrick and others. The twelve apostles were Christ's inner circle, people he personally chose from amongst his disciples; thus they will be given special consideration in this chapter.

The twelve apostles are traditionally recounted as (Matthew 10): 1. **Peter** (Simon Peter), 2. **Andrew**, 3. **James** (son of Zebedee), 4. **John** (his brother), 5. **Philip**, 6. **Bartholomew**, 7. **Thomas,** and 8. **Matthew** (the publican), 9. **James** (son of Alphaeus), and 10. Lebbaeus **Thaddeus**. Plus, 11. **Simon** (the Zealot), and 12. **Judas** Iscariot. The Gospel of Matthew follows Mark, and Luke substitutes Jude for Mark's Thaddeus. John refers to the twelve and includes the name Nathanael. In the Synoptic gospels we see special attention given to certain apostles: Jesus' brother James is given charge to preside over the church in Jerusalem. Peter is specifically mentioned as a cornerstone of the new church. Thomas is also given special attention, as are John and Mary Magdalene. After Judas Iscariot betrays Christ and kills himself, **Matthias** is voted in as the apostle to replace Judas (Acts 1), thus completing the twelve.

Years later Saul, who converts to Christianity, changes his name from the Jewish Saul to the pagan Paul and claims the role of apostle to the Gentiles—a thirteenth apostle. Paul had previously not known the apostles or Jesus nor had the benefit of studying with them, but after seeing the light on the road to Damascus to persecute Christians he hears the Lord speak to him and was inspired to accept Jesus and to preach his understanding of the gospel. Paul's theological development and contributions will be addressed in a later chapter, but for the sake of discussing what I am calling the apostles' canon I am referring to those apostles who (1) walked physically with Jesus, (2) were recognized as leaders in his movement, and (3) we have credible physical texts of their gospels dating to the first and early second centuries; I am excluding the later Christian Gnostic writings that appear in later centuries as they are historically not authentic, but they will be discussed in the following chapter.

One of the most striking facts about the New Testament is that even though it tells us that Christ chose twelve apostles to preach the good news (which is what *gospel* means), there are only four gospels in the New Testament: Matthew, Mark, Luke and John. Where are all the others? What is even more striking is that neither Luke nor Mark are listed as original apostles (they came later). Of the original twelve apostles, only Matthew and John have gospels in the New Testament. One might conclude that the other apostles either didn't have gospels or that they no longer exist, but this is not the case. The gospels of Peter, James, Thomas, Philip, Judas, and Mary all existed in the centuries before the formation of the church's canon and were read widely by Christians in their day. There were also many Gnostic spin offs, and adapted versions of Christ's teachings introduced to pagan religions that all get clumped into this category called Gnosticism.

Most of what is referred to as Gnosticism today are these later ideas developed more than a century after Christ that began to go off into theologies that were not necessarily what Christ taught. This muddles any discussion of early Christian theology, so in this chapter we are going to focus on those gospels that 1) are attributed to actual apostles that Christ picked, and 2) were written years before the Council of Nicea and the formation of the Church's canon, and are not already included in the New Testament. Thus, what I am defining as the apostles' canon includes Thomas, James, Philip, and I am adding Mary Magdalene as she becomes acknowledged as a special apostle of Christ. Here we find a treasure of Christ's teachings that provide us a wealth of insights into Christ's message; herein lies some of the world's greatest spiritual teachings.

New Testament Apostles

Matthew holds a prominent position because the gospel attributed to him is the first book in the New Testament. Matthew means gift of Yahweh (God), and he is credited with writing the Gospel According to Matthew, although the actual authorship is not attested to in the gospel itself. The oldest copy of the gospel does not include the last two chapters of the gospel, which talk about Christ's Ascension or the virgin birth, so it is believed that those chapters were added later when the text was translated to Greek. By tradition Matthew is also identified with Levi, the publican or tax collector mentioned by Mark. Of all the New Testament gospels, Matthew keeps closest to the Jewish traditions and is most similar to the Apostles canon.

The only other apostle appointed by Christ directly whose gospel appears in the New Testament is **John**. John was the son of Zebedee and brother of Saint James the Greater. The Eastern Orthodox tradition identifies his mother as Salome. Originally the whole family were fishermen in the Lake of Genesareth, and he was first a disciple of John the Baptist. John sits next to Jesus at the last supper before his trial and crucifixion (John 13:23-25), accompanies Peter to make preparation for the Passover meal (Luke 22:8), and is the only male apostle present at the Crucifixion of Christ. He takes care of Mary on Jesus' behalf (John 19:25-27), and he is one of the most active in founding and guiding the church in those first few formative years.

One of the biggest debates during the Council of Nicea was whether John the apostle was the same John who wrote **Revelation**. Historians generally agree that the author of the Gospel of John and the author of Revelation are different individuals, as the writing style of each book is so different. Church fathers debated including Revelation in the Bible at the Council of Nicea, and they were not all in agreement. That debate continued for hundreds of years and Revelation was never accepted or included in either the Coptic (Egyptian) or Ethiopian Bibles, neither was it in the original Aramaic Bible, but only included later. There is no evidence that the first Jewish Christians used Revelation either. Moreover, the basic storyline of Revelation comes right out of the Old Testament book of Daniel. For instance, in Daniel 7:1-8, it states that Daniel had a dream, in that dream four beasts came out of the sea, one had features of a lion with eagles wings, a second was like that of a bear, another like a leopard, and the next had ten horns on its head. These images are understood to be metaphorical and not meant to be taken literally. In Revelation 13:1 John has a vision, and in this vision a beast comes out of the sea, it too has ten horns, the likeness of a leopard, the feet of a bear, the mouth of a lion and wings. The church fathers originally understood these images to be metaphorical too, but during the Middle Ages these images were taken literally and used to generate great fear among the congregants, and many Christians today still take this story literally.

Very little is known about **Jude**, also identified with Jude of James, Jude Thaddeus or Thaddeus, or the apostle **Bartholomew**, but both are honored by the Armenian Church, which suggests that these saints or their disciples brought the way to Armenia (where they would have used the Peshitta). Little is known about **Simon**, also known as Simon Zelotes or Simon the Zealot, except that he was identified with the Jewish Zealot movement to rebel against the Roman empire and take possession of their land back. **Judas Iscariot**, "the traitor" was also a Zealot, but his gospel has very recently been dug up out of the desert and translated to English and will be addressed in a following chapter. **Andrew** was, along with his older brother **Peter**, the first to be called by Jesus to become "fishers of men" or apostles. **Matthias** was chosen by the other eleven apostles (Acts 1:18-26) after the crucifixion to replace Judas, as Judas had betrayed Christ by giving information about Jesus' whereabouts to the Romans who captured him to stand trial and be crucified, and afterward Judas kills himself.

The Apostles **Thomas, James, Philip,** and **Peter** all have gospels that date back to the first and second centuries, as well as the *secret* Gospel of John. So centuries before the development of the New Testament canon, Christ's closest apostles had evangelized as Jesus had asked, their words were recorded and their gospels shared among the Christian communities for centuries. These *lost* gospels were used primarily by the Jewish followers of Jesus, the God fearers (Gentiles who had taken an interest in Judaism) and those living in the areas of Israel and Egypt, the Aramaic-speaking lands of Syria, Mesopotamia, and Persia, extending as far as India. The Pauline scriptures were more popular with the pagan Greek and Roman cultures in modern Turkey, Greece and Italy.

According to biblical scholars, these first Christians were seeking higher knowledge and to know God. In Marvin W. Meyer's *The Secret Teachings of Jesus* he summarizes their perspective of God as "a completely good and transcendent God, whose enlightened greatness is utterly unfathomable and essentially indescribable. Yet this divine Other can be experienced in a person's inner life, for the spirit within is actually the divine self, the inner spark or ray of heavenly light." Humans had fallen asleep and forgotten their divine nature, what the Kabbalists call our "spark of divinity," and this is what Christ was awakening. Meyers, who is cochair of the Department of Religious Studies at Chapman University and a leading expert on early Christianity goes on to explain how the early Christians were going to find God's kingdom:

> **In order to be liberated, then, the spirit needs to be awakened and brought sobriety, wholeness, knowledge, and enlightenment.**

What the early Christians were seeking was an awakening of the spirit and enlightenment of consciousness. The transformation was from within; God was within and without, and each individual was to realize God for himself or herself. The early Christians sought God realization, and Jesus was enlightening them. These first Gnostic Christians tended to retreat to the desert and practiced various forms of meditation, contemplation, and prayer, and their firsthand accounts of the gospels was written down and studied. And now we can too. A voice that had been silenced for over 2,000 years now speaks to us.

The Apostle Thomas

Didymus Judas Thomas was one of Jesus' closest apostles; also known as Didymus (the twin) or Doubting Thomas (because at first he didn't believe Christ has risen from the tomb). The Syrian Church and older traditions believe that Thomas was a blood brother of Jesus. Thomas appears in a few passages in the Gospel of John (14:5) when he questions Jesus during the last supper about where he will be going, and (11:16) when the apostles are resisting Jesus' decision to return to Judea because the Jews there had tried to stone him to death, Thomas says bravely "Let us also go, that we might die with him," as martyrdom is an honor in the Middle East. Thomas traveled outside the Roman Empire, preaching and establishing churches in Persia and India, where his church continues to this day. There are two valuable works to explore from Thomas: The Gospel of Thomas and the Book of Thomas the Contender (the Acts of Thomas is a third century Gnostic text indicative of movements that transpired later and is not germane to our discussion here).

The Gospel of Thomas

The Gospel of Thomas is one of the most sensational archaeological discoveries of the twentieth century; moreover this Coptic papyrus manuscript that was discovered in 1945 is nearly completely preserved. When the complete version of Thomas was found, scholars realized that three separate portions of a Greek version of it had already been discovered in Oxyrhynchus, Egypt, dating to around 200 CE. Scholars believe the original version dates back as early as 60 CE or as late as 140 CE, making it one of the oldest of all the gospels. Rather than a narrative like the synoptic gospels, Thomas' gospel is a collection of quotes of Jesus. This gospel does not include a narrative of his life or any references to his immaculate conception, his ascension, or any mention of redemption from original sin, but it does provide a wealth of information about Christ's teachings. The Gospel of Thomas contains 114 sayings of Jesus Christ, approximately half of which also appear in the Synoptic gospels (Matthew, Mark and Luke). These sayings are the most instructive of Christ's teachings to his apostles and give us greater clarity as to the meaning of Christ's cryptic metaphors and messages.

The Gospel of Thomas is unique in that Thomas states in the opening lines of the book that he himself heard Jesus make these statements and then wrote them down himself. As scholars recognize that the older the scripture is, the closer to the time Jesus actually spoke these words, the more reliable the work can be; as generations pass there is a greater chance of errors in translation, editing, additions, or that it is a forgery. In the Gospel of Thomas, we find several saying that also appear in the New Testament: Verse 20, the parable of the mustard seed (Mark 4:30-31). Verse 26, removing the speck from your brother's eye (Matthew 7:3-5). Verse 34, the blind leading the blind (Matthew 15:14), and Verse 54, blessed are the poor (Luke 6:20). In the Gospel of Thomas, these saying are shorter and pithier than their New Testament counterparts, which has led historians to conclude they were written first, and were expanded upon in the Synoptic Gospels years later.

Thus, the Gospel of Thomas is unique in that is likely older than the other gospels, with the possible exception of an early version of Matthew, or Mary, and it was written by an actual apostle of Christ. There is evidence that Thomas was in wide use amongst the first Jewish Christians in the first century. In short, it's closer to Jesus' own words than any of Paul or Luke's writings, and thus deserves our close attention and study. In the introduction, Thomas begins by quoting what Jesus is saying to his disciples, verse 1 (using Dr. Marvin Meyer's translation):

> **Whoever finds the interpretation of these sayings will not taste death.**

This statement is a classic explanation of how an inner realization provides transcendence of consciousness, when the true nature of the self is realized the temporal physical body is seen as only a garment (that can be discarded) while the spirit that we are never dies. Thus when you come to know your own nature, you transcend physical death. The focus here is not on belief or faith but, rather, on enlightenment.

Verse 2, Jesus said:

> Let him who seeks continue seeking until he finds. When he finds, he will become troubled. When he becomes troubled, he will be astonished, and he will rule over all.

Clearly Jesus is encouraging us to seek, to look within, and realize the truth for ourselves. When you discover the truth it can be *troubling* for we tend to be very attached to our old ideas and beliefs, but as the truth becomes revealed it is beyond comprehension, it's *astonishing*. When you realize your true nature you are no longer subjugated by the trammels of your own mind or senses, or influences by others who are still asleep; you have greater awareness—*you rule over all*.

Verse 3, Jesus said:

> If those who lead you say to you, 'See, the kingdom is in the sky,' then the birds of the sky will precede you. If they say to you, 'It is in the sea,' then the fish will precede you. Rather, the kingdom is inside of you, and it is outside of you.

Clearly, Jesus is explaining that the kingdom of heaven is not some physical place out there but rather a state of consciousness that is realized through self-reflection. Like a mirror that reflects an image of our face, as we reflect on our own nature, it becomes clear to our own mind. This principal is not just in the Gospel of Thomas, or other lost codex's, it's also in the New Testament. In Luke (17:21) Jesus tells his disciples "Neither shall they say, Lo here! or, lo there! for behold, **the kingdom of God is within you.**"

Then Jesus goes on to clarify the way to finding the kingdom in Thomas:

> **When you come to know yourselves, then you will become known, and you will realize that it is you who are the sons of the living father. But if you will not know yourselves you dwell in poverty and it is you who are in poverty.**

We are to look within and come to know ourselves. Jesus is teaching the path to self-realization. When Jesus states "it is you who are the sons of the living father" he is helping us to see the true nature of our own being. We, too, are the sons of the living father, we too are his children. Jesus is guiding us home, back to our father, but the path lies within us. We need to turn our awareness around 180 degrees and become conscious of that which is conscious of itself. Through self-awareness we find the kingdom inside; we find the kingdom within. It's a state of consciousness in which you realize God; God dwelling within you and around you, everywhere, all the time. This is paradise.

In *Beyond Belief: The Secret Gospel of Thomas*, Elaine Pagels, professor of religion at Princeton University, first quotes from Professor MacRae's translation of The Gospel of Thomas: "Jesus said: 'If you bring forth what is within you, what you bring forth will save you. If you do not bring forth what is within you, what you do not bring forth will destroy you.'" And then she goes on to point out that: "The strength of this saying is that it does not tell us what to believe but challenges us to discover what lies hidden within ourselves."

Then, in the verse 6, the disciples are questioning him as to which of their laws and customs they should follow and Jesus clarifies the way to them:

> **Do you want us to fast? How shall we pray? Shall we give alms? What diet shall we observe? Jesus said, do not tell lies, and do not do what you hate, for all things are plain in the sight of heaven. For nothing covered will remain without being uncovered.**

So here we see Jesus is guiding his disciples away from the old institutional and dogmatic instruction and observances, and into more personal accountability. He is teaching us to become more conscious of what we say and do, and to take personal responsibility for our thoughts and actions and be mindful of how our actions affect others. He is making a very clear distinction of not going outside of yourself for the answers and not blindly following religious leaders or the rules they create, but, rather, to go within to that part of you that already knows right from wrong.

Thomas then goes on to recount other messages of Christ that we also hear in the New Testament, such as the "Sower of seeds metaphor" (Matthew 13:18). Approximately half of what is collected in the Gospel of Thomas also appears in the New Testament, but it's the new information that is most interesting and exciting. Jesus then further explains the nature of our eternal being.

Verse 11, Jesus said:

> **This heaven will pass away, and the one above it will pass away. The dead are not alive, and the living will not die. In the days when you consumed what is dead, you made it what is alive. When you come to dwell in the light, what will you do? On the day when you were one you became two. But when you become two, what will you do?**

These references to "this heaven" and the "one above it" are references to concepts explained in the Jewish Kabbalah, where heaven is regarded as a state of total consciousness. Lower states of consciousness are represented by duality: physical body and consciousness. As soon as we appear to incarnate into physical form there appears to be separation between our mind and our consciousness; you appear to become two and separate from your own divine nature.

In verse 12 the disciples ask Jesus: "We know that you will depart from us. Who is to be our leader?" Jesus makes it very clear, when he says:

"Wherever you are, you are to go to James the righteous (Just), for whose sake heaven and earth came into being." So, where Peter and John play key roles in the Jesus movement, along with Paul years later, Jesus makes clear that James and his followers are to lead the church.

In verse 13 Jesus asks his disciples whom he (Christ) is like? Simon Peter says, "You are like a righteous angel," Matthew says "You are like a wise philosopher," and then Thomas says "Master, my mouth is wholly incapable of saying whom you are like." Whereupon, Jesus replies to him "I am not your master. Because you have drunk, you have **become intoxicated from the bubbling spring which I have measured out.**" In stating that he is not Thomas's master and that he has become "drunk" on what he has measured out, Christ is explaining what happens when you are in the presence of a true master. In the East they call the experience of feeling intoxicated by being in the presence of an enlightened master *Darshan*. Christ's spirit body invokes a spring of life force energy called *Shaktipat* in the Eastern spiritual vernacular, and those who are in the presence of a great master, will feel this divine energy "bubbling up" from within providing a blissful state of awareness called *Layla Samadhi*. You feel the presence of God around those who have realized God. By stating that he (Christ) was not his master, he is acknowledging that Thomas has joined him in consciousness. They are one in spirit and consciousness—they are undivided. You are at one with the father, just as "the father and I are one."

Jesus then takes Thomas to have some private time with him, and when he returns the disciples ask him, "What did Jesus say to you?" Whereupon, Thomas replied "If I tell you one of the things which he told me, you will pick up stones and throw them at me; a fire will come out of the stones and burn you up." Why would the disciples be so angry with him that they would throw stones? We don't know, but it appears clear that Christ is acknowledging his higher state of realization, and it appears that that special recognition might cause resentment. He appears to get it whereas the other's still have not. But what is he getting? What is Christ offering?

Verse 17, Jesus said:

> I shall give you what no eye has seen and what no ear has heard and what no hand has touched and what has never occurred to the human mind.

In other words he will guide us to that which is transcendental; he will enlighten us. What lies beyond? They desire to behold the mystery. The disciples then ask Jesus "how their end shall be," and in verse 18 he explains by asking a question of the disciples:

> Have you discovered, then, the beginning, that you look for the end? For where the beginning is, there will be the end. Blessed is he who will take his place in the beginning; he will know the end and will not experience death.

Follow your thoughts back to their source and your consciousness moves out of the realm of time and space, and there is no beginning or end. This is an eternal truth passed on through many ancient spiritual traditions. To take your place "in the beginning" is to step back from your mind and observe it. What is there before thought? That which observes the mind is eternal—your consciousness is eternal. Consciousness transcends time, space, energy, and matter. In consciousness there is no beginning or end—this is the eternal nature of our own being. Jesus is teaching one of the great secrets: Your true nature is eternal.

In verse 22 Jesus sees infants being suckled by their mothers and says to his disciples, "These infants being suckled are like those who enter the kingdom." Whereupon, the disciples then ask him, "Shall we then, as children, enter the Kingdom?" And Jesus says to them:

> When you make the two one, and when you make the inside like the outside and the outside like the inside, and the above like the below, and when you make the male and the female one and the same, so that the male not be male nor female female; and when you fashion eyes in place of an eye, and a hand in place of a hand, and a foot in place of a foot, and a likeness in place of a likeness; then will you enter the kingdom.

This discussion of making two one, and inside like the outside, and male and female as one, replacing a likeness with a likeness are all ways of describing the nonduality of our own intrinsic higher nature. Yogic and Buddhist philosophies also describe such nonduality, as does the Kabbalah. What we are is not male or female, but consciousness itself, formless and unchanging. When you "make the two one," is a universal spiritual truth that refers to entering the nondifferentiated state of total consciousness. When the inside is like the outside and the outside like the inside you have become enlightened. In verse 61 Jesus describes himself: "I am he who exists from the undivided"; in other words, he is enlightened. But he is not bragging; he's explaining how we can join him.

In verse 24 the disciples ask Jesus, "Show us the place where you are, since it is necessary for us to seek it," and Jesus tells them:

> Whoever has ears, let them hear. There is a light within a man of light, and he lights up the whole world. If he does not shine, he is darkness.

The light is within us. Jesus keeps explaining to his disciples to go within for the answers—not a special diet or fasting, not reading scripture or listening to bishops, not looking outside of oneself for the answers. Just as we see our physical form through a reflection, as we reflect upon our own nature it too becomes clear for our own mind to see. Through meditation your mind becomes clear like a placid lake, and reflects back to you your own eternal nature.

In both the church canon and the apostles' canon we read how Jesus is trying to help his disciples realize who he really is. To see who he is we must look beyond his form. In verse 37 the disciples ask him, "When will you become revealed to us and when shall we see you?" And Jesus said:

> **When you disrobe without being ashamed and take up your garments and place them under your feet like little children and tread on them, then you will see the son of the living one, and you will not be afraid.**

In this esoteric language, *garments* refers to our earthly bodies. Your spirit is like a child, and when you set it fee, through enlightenment, you will see the son of man in everyone and in everything and will not be afraid. Jesus goes further to explain in language similar to the New Testament (Matt. 18:4, Mark 10:15, Luke 18:17) in Thomas verse 46 it states: "whichever one of you comes to be a child will be acquainted with the Kingdom and will be superior to John."

Throughout the apostles canon Jesus speaks of the kingdom as being something that is accessible in the present moment, with him, and through him. It appears Thomas had found it already, but the others were still grasping for it at this point. So they ask the Lord in verse 51, "When will the new world come?" Christ's answer is one of the most important secrets revealed in all biblical literature:

> **What you look forward to has already come, but you do not recognize it.**

The kingdom has come. It is a state of consciousness in which you realize the living presence of God within you and around you, in everything, everywhere, all the time. This is God realization or enlightenment. We are to look within and discover our own nature to realize the kingdom of heaven on earth. In verse 111 Jesus says, "Whoever finds himself is superior to the world." Then Jesus explains what the kingdom of heaven or enlightenment is in what I believe to be the most profound pronouncement from any of the world's great spiritual teachings. In verse 113 the disciples ask Jesus "When will the Kingdom come?" To which Jesus replies:

> It will not come by waiting for it. It will not be a matter of saying "here it is" or "there it is." Rather, the kingdom of the father is spread out upon the earth, and men do not see it.

Those that have eyes let them see "it is spread out upon the earth, and men do not see it." Heaven is not beyond the planet Pluto or the big bang, it is right here on earth. The kingdom of heaven is a state of consciousness in which you realize God; it is a state of enlightenment. This is Christ's teachings on the way to enlightenment and God realization—heaven on earth.

In *Beyond Belief: The Secret Gospel of Thomas*, Elaine Pagels explains the early Christian perspective of salvation as "that the divine light Jesus embodied is shared by humanity, since we are all made 'in the image of God.' Thus Thomas expresses what would become a central theme of Jewish - and later Christian - mysticism a thousand years later; that the 'image of God' is hidden within everyone, although, most people remain unaware of its presence." In other words, Jesus is clarifying that we are the same in consciousness, same in spirit, but not same in physical form. Moreover, we are to seek him within. Jesus is guiding us to self-reflection, contemplation, and meditation; he is helping us to realize the presence of God within us and around us. Jesus says "It **will not come by waiting for it.**" It's not going to come some day; it has come, and it is "**spread out before us**." In other words, it's **here and now**. The divine presence is present to all those who have the presence of mind to look for it. The more you look, the more you will see; but the looking is within according to Jesus.

The Book of Thomas the Contender

The Book of Thomas (the Contender) is also one of the oldest of the gospels ever discovered; followers of Thomas in India use a rendition they believe dates to before 52 CE, when their church was founded. A copy is also included in the Nag Hammadi Library cache of papyrus scriptures recently discovered in Egypt. The book is part dialog and part monologue, and imparts more of Christ's inner teachings to his disciples. The book begins with the declaration "The secret words that the savior spoke to Judas Thomas which I, even I, Mathaias, wrote down, while I was walking, listening to them speak to one another." So it appears that this Matthias would likely be the Matthias who was voted in as the twelfth apostle after Judas, who was apparently acting as the secretary writing down what Jesus said. This is what the savior said:

> **Brother Thomas, while you have time in the world, listen to me, and I will reveal to you the things you have pondered in your mind. Now since it has been said that you are my twin and true companion, examine yourself and learn who you are, in what way you exist, and how you will come to be.**

So now Jesus is making it very clear that the way lies through introspection —"examine yourself." We are to reflect on our own nature; he instructs us to "learn who you are" like all the great yogis. He asks us "in what way do you exist," meaning what is that which causes our existence, and what underlies the essence of our own being? What is that within us that causes us to exist? Meditation and introspection are the path: "Examine yourself and learn who you are." Self-realization is coming to know the true nature of your self, and this is exactly what Jesus was teaching. The emphasis is on turning one's awareness inward and attaining a *realization*. In the East this practice of introspection is called Jhana Yoga or Vedanta. Christ was a Jewish yogi; the whole emphasis of his teaching in the first century was introspection, contemplation, and meditation. It's not about sin, hell, or redemption, it's about realization of self and God. Christ goes on to say:

> Since you are called my brother, it is not fitting that you be ignorant of yourself. And I know that you have understood, because you had already understood that I am the knowledge of the truth. So while you accompany me, although you are uncomprehending, you have already come to know, and you will be called "the one who knows himself." For he who has not known himself has known nothing, but he who has known himself has at the same time already achieved knowledge about the depth of the all.

One who knows himself is self realized; as you are made in the image of God, you realize what God is and attain God realization. When one becomes enlightened one enters the kingdom of heaven on earth. When you have realized your true nature as spirit, you enter a world of spirit. As you realize the spirit within you as you, you begin to see it in everyone else and in everything, everywhere, all the time. You are never separate from it because it is you. Your awareness of God's presence within you and around you becomes undifferentiated, and that divine union is blissful beyond description.

The kingdom of heaven is already upon us—we have only to open our eyes to see. That which causes life within you is you. You've never been anything other than that which you are, but you are not your body and mind; you are an expression of consciousness we call spirit. We are all spirit; there is a whole world of spirit present on earth, but most people live in ignorance of it. Jesus is showing us how to see through the mind's eye to behold the presence of God on earth. Christ invites us to set our spirit free and take off our *garments* and dance like children in paradise…here on earth…now. The one who knows himself is Christ Enlightened.

The Saint Thomas Christians of India

As each apostle had a mission to spread the good news to the world, they spread out into different lands. Thomas traveled to Persia and then India. In the first century the southwestern coast of India was a growing trading area for teak, ivory, spices, and other goods, and trade routes had already been well established between India and the Mediterranean through Israel. Some of the earliest settlements of the Jewish Diaspora were along this Malabar Coast in the state of Kerala, in southwest India. These "Malabar Jews" developed strong relationships between India and Israel, and travel and trade were well established in the first century. In a third century scripture called the Acts of Thomas we learn that Thomas has already started a church in Kerala along the Malabar Coast of southwest India in 52 CE. This provides further evidence that Thomas's writings were likely written before 52 CE. This church is still flourishing today in a line of succession from the first century; they are called the Syrian Malabar Nasranis or Saint Thomas Christians. Here is another a living link (in addition to the Aramaic speaking Mesopotamian Christians) to the original teachings of Jesus Christ.

The **Syrian Malabar Nasranis** are Syrian as to their physical origin and language (Syrian dialect of Aramaic) and were Hebrews who migrated to India. Over generations their Semitic bloodlines have intermixed with locals, and their traditions have adapted to the Hindu culture, but they are still true to their Jewish-Christian roots. Malabar is the coast along the Kerala state of Southern India, and Nasranis are the Jewish Christians. Their symbol is the Nasranj Menorah, with a Christian Cross sitting on top of a Jewish Menorah. An Indian epic from the Tamil tradition called the *Manimekkalai* mentions that the Nasranis were called Essenes. So here again we see a link connecting Essene Jews with Christianity. Marco Polo mentions the Nasrani Christians of India in his travels, as do many of the church fathers, including, Origen, Eusebius, and Ephrem.

Moreover, the Saint Thomas Christians have their own records dating back to the first century and recorded Saint Thomas' founding a church there. They use the Book of Thomas and continue to maintain the Jewish tradition, such as, keeping the Jewish Sabbath and observing the high holidays, but they also believe that Jesus is the Messiah. The Saint Thomas Christians are Gnostic; they believe that salvation comes from within and seek enlightenment through Jesus. Their liturgies were in Aramaic until the 1970s and some hymns are still sung in the Aramaic-Syriac language, Jesus' own native tongue. There are now over five million Nasrani Christians spread out throughout India. Since, neither the Roman Empire nor the Orthodox Church stretched as far as southern India, they have been able to carry on with their traditions unmolested for over two thousand years, although Portuguese missionaries converted many years later. The way is alive and well in India.

The Apostle James

The Apostle James, also known as "James the Just" and "the Brother of the Lord," was the leader or bishop of the church based in Jerusalem. James was Jesus Christ's blood brother. In Matthew (13:55) and in Mark (6:3) and Galatians (1:19) Jesus' brothers are named as James, Jude, Simon, and Joses, and James is always mentioned first, which suggests he would be the eldest of Jesus' siblings; the fact that Jesus had sisters is also mentioned. In Josephus' *Jewish Antiquities* (20.9.1), James is described as "the brother of Jesus who is called Christ." The word being used to describe brother here, according to the experts, clearly means *blood brother*, as opposed to being a friend or stepbrother. Later, as the pagan concept of immaculate conception (virgin birth) was introduced, and this definition of James being a brother was explained as James being Jesus' step-brother, half-brother, cousin, or close associate to make sense of this contradiction, but it isn't true. In the Eastern Church, James is referred to as "James Adelphotheos" or "James the Brother of God." Early Christians believed both Jesus and James were blood brothers whose parents were Mary and Joseph, but these accounts were revised in the Greco-Roman church because the mythological hero's of these pagans all had immaculate conceptions, as you will see.

James was regarded as being the leader of the early church. When Peter miraculously escapes from prison and flees Herod Agrippa's persecution, he asks that James be informed (Acts 12:17). When Paul and Barnabas come to a special counsel of the apostles to petition that Gentiles be excluded from circumcision and observance of Mosaic laws and Jewish customs (Acts 15:13), it is James who has the last word and agrees with most of the repeals but insists on not allowing followers to eat meat offered to idols or engage in fornication. When Paul delivers the money he has raised from the Gentiles during a drought in Jerusalem, he delivers it to James (Acts 21:18), and Jesus himself makes it clear in the Gospel of Thomas that he is putting James, not Peter, at the head of the church. It is also James who insists that Paul ritually cleanse himself at the temple to prove his faith and deny rumors that his teachings are against the Bible (Acts 21:18). In the earlier gospels, it is clear that Jesus has made James the leader of his movement, yet the orthodox church fathers decide centuries later to leave out his gospel because it competes with the authority of the church in Rome, which emphasizes Paul's writings and had become much larger than the Jewish and Aramaic sects by the end of the second century.

Saint Jerome, in his *De Viris Illustribus*, quotes **Hegesippus'** (an early Christian chronicler) account of James from his book *Commentaries* (which is now lost), from the third century:

> After the apostles, James the brother of the Lord surnamed the Just was made head of the Church at Jerusalem. Many indeed are called James. This one was holy from his mother's (Mary's) womb. He drank neither wine nor strong drink, ate no flesh, never shaved or anointed himself with ointment or bathed. He alone had the privilege of entering the Holy of Holies, since indeed he did not use woolen vestments but linen and went alone into the temple and prayed in behalf of the people, insomuch that his knees were reputed to have acquired the hardness of camels' knees.

As the only Jews allowed in the "Holy of Holies" were high priests of the temple (and only on the Jewish holiday of atonement Yom Kippur), this has led scholars to believe that James must have been a high priest. But as leader of the church after Christ's Crucifixion, those who hated Jesus went after James. In Clement of Alexandria's *Historica Ecclesiae* (2.23), Clement quotes Hegesippus as saying that the scribes and Pharisees went to James to petition him to help put down the Jesus movement:

> They came, therefore, in a body to James and said: "We entreat thee, restrain the people: for they are gone astray in their opinions about Jesus. We entreat thee to persuade all who have come hither for the day of the Passover, concerning Jesus. For we all listen to thy persuasion; since we, as well as all the people, bear thee testimony that thou art just, and showest partiality to none."

To the dismay of the scribes and Pharisees, James boldly testifies that Christ "Himself sitteth in heaven, at the right hand of the Great Power, and shall come on the clouds of heaven." The "Great Power" was the way those following the way described God. This term for God is used in the Kabbalah and was also adopted by the Gnostics later. This account goes on further to state that upon hearing this, the mob threw James from a cliff, but as that didn't quite kill him, they then stoned him to death:

> [T]hrew down the just man…began to stone him: for he was not killed by the fall; but he turned, and kneeled down, and said: "I beseech Thee, Lord God our Father, forgive them; for they know not what they do."

In addition to the Epistle of James in the New Testament, we also have the Apocryphon of James from the Nag Hammadi Library, as well as later works, such as, the First and Second Apocalypse of James and the Protoevangelium of James or infancy gospel, which describe Jesus' childhood, but they were written later and hold less historical authenticity and will be discussed in the next chapter along with the Gnostic and Greek embellishments. James kept closer to Mosaic laws and Jewish customs and to the study of self-awareness as you shall see.

The Apocryphon of James

The Book of James, also known as the Apocryphon of James or The Secret Book of James is attributed to James the Just, Jesus' brother and first bishop of Jerusalem. It describes the secret teachings that Jesus gave to Peter and James. This codex is believed to have been written sometime before 150 CE. James shares what Christ revealed to Peter and him about how to attain the kingdom. Jesus is directing his disciples to come into the kingdom through their own realization. He tells them "no one will ever enter the kingdom of heaven at my bidding, but only because you yourselves are full." You must look within and realize God for yourself.

In James, Christ is explaining to his disciples that to realize your true nature you must sacrifice your own ego identity. As you awaken, you transcend your own personal wants, needs, and desires, and you become more selfless (like Jesus), as the ego sense of *I* expires. Your true nature is eternal; it never expires. Jesus tells us to become "seekers of death" for "when you examine death it will teach you election." Jesus said:

> **Verily I say unto you, none of those who fear death will be saved; for the kingdom of God belongs to those who put themselves to death. Become better than I; make yourselves like the son of the Holy Spirit!**

In other words, realize your true nature as spirit for whereas your body will die your spirit is eternal. This ego death, or transcendence from the trammels of the mind and senses, is the path to liberation from birth and death, which is enlightenment by any other name. Then Jesus shares with us how to attain it:

> For this cause I tell you this, that you may know yourselves. For the kingdom of heaven is like an ear of grain after it has sprouted in the field. And when it had ripened, it scattered its fruit and again filled the field with ears for another year. You also, hasten to reap an ear of life for yourselves that you may be filled with the kingdom.

So, again, we get clarity from Christ that heaven is not some place out there but a state of consciousness that lies within us. This consciousness grows as you become conscious of it; as you nurture your consciousness, by putting attention on it, it develops. Consciousness develops as you become ever more conscious of your consciousness. Jesus goes on to tell them, "Do not make the kingdom of heaven a desert within you." You must cultivate this higher awareness, just like tending crops. Awareness grows with your attention, as you till and feed it. Then Jesus departs from his apostles telling them:

> But I have said my last word to you, and I shall depart from you, for the chariot of spirit has borne me aloft, and from this moment on I shall strip myself that I may clothe myself.

So here we gain some understanding of the cryptic messages we keep hearing as Jesus, like in the Old Testament, conveys his messages in metaphor and uses analogies to impart concepts. His metaphors are not meant to be read literally—you would completely miss the point taking the meaning literally. He is trying to convey what is beyond comprehension, so Jesus is using metaphors and guided imagery. The "chariot" is a Kabalistic metaphor for spirit, and he is stripping himself of his earthly physical garment (his body) to clothe himself in the light of his own indwelling spirit. Christ is teaching the Kabbalah. And then he tells them:

> And I pray that the beginning may come from you, for thus I shall be capable of salvation, since they will be enlightened through me.

The Apostle Philip

Philip was one of the original twelve apostles who followed Jesus and evangelized until he was martyred by crucifixion in the city of Hierapolis. He is not to be confused with Philip the Evangelist mentioned in the Acts of the Apostles. The Gospel of John describes Philip's calling as a disciple of Jesus (John 1:43) and says that he is from the same town as Andrew and Peter, Bethsaida. The Gospel of John also tells us how Philip introduces Nathaniel (sometimes identified with Bartholomew) to Jesus (John 1:45-47). Moreover, Philip introduces members of his community to Jesus (John 12:20-36) and spreads the gospel in his own town. So he was clearly an active apostle and part of Christ's inner circle. The church father Clement further tells us that Philip was married and had children, including a daughter who was married.

The Gospel of Philip

The Gospel of Philip was discovered in Nag Hammadi, Egypt, and is dated between 180-350 CE. Philip's gospel addresses the sacraments (of baptism, unction, and marriage), as well as diving deeper into the origin and nature of mankind and the path to enlightenment. In Philip, we see Jesus using metaphor again to explain the secrets of the universe, and Philip uses the sacred union of man and women in sexual intercourse as a metaphor to explain the nature of man's union with the Holy Spirit. The "bridal chamber" is used to describe the sacred place where you make union with God. As individual spirit joins and merges with the Holy Spirit, the two become one; individual consciousness merges with total consciousness, and the One is realized. In fact, we have never been separated from our Creator, and this is what is realized in our own mind.

In Philip we learn more of Christ's yogic teachings on nonduality and learn transcendence over the passions of the mind. Judgments create duality; the mind creates opposites, and the senses differentiate, but the consciousness is unchanging and remains the same. Here, Jesus is on record as saying to the Christians of Israel:

> Light and darkness, life and death, right and left, are brothers of one another. They are inseparable. Because of this neither are the good good, nor the evil evil, nor is life life, nor death death. For this reason each one will dissolve into the earliest origin. But those who are exalted above the world are indissoluble, eternal.

As the disciples are having difficulty trying to comprehend the incomprehensible, Jesus explains the self-reflective quality of consciousness to them. He guides his followers to look beyond their eyes and expand their awareness beyond the faculties of their mind and senses to realize the eternal nature of their own being. All appearances are temporal and fleeting, and not ultimately real; what is eternal, unchanging, and present is real. Duality of senses creates an illusion that the mind takes to be real. Our ideas of good and evil are created in our mind, and what we think we project into our mind's sense of reality. In other words, our own mind distorts reality depending on what beliefs you hold. Your consciousness must transcend the trammels of the mind and senses in order to realize God. Our minds are like instruments that are only calibrated to measure a small gradation of the divine expression we call life. This is why we meditate—to be present with the eternal presence, the undifferentiated whole. The consciousness itself is unfettered, undivided, and whole. Only the mind creates divisions, conflict, and the illusion of being separate from God. This delusion of separation from God is man's fall from grace, which is the underlying cause of mankind's suffering. Our mind creates a sense of *I* that distinguishes us from our true nature, which is always with the Father—Abba. Jesus further explains:

> It is not possible for anyone to see anything of the things that actually exist unless he becomes like them. This is not the way with man in the world; he sees the sun without being a sun; and he sees the heaven and earth and all other things, but he is not these things. This is quite in keeping with the truth.

What is real is eternal, unchanging, and undifferentiated; what is -temporal and fleeting is unreal. As long as we keep looking outside of ourselves, through our mind and senses, we only see the illusion of being separate from God, but when you go within and see who you are, then all becomes revealed, like stepping back from a microscope. The world around you is a reflection of your state of consciousness, and your state of consciousness is reflected in how you see the world. Jesus goes on further to explain this:

> **You saw the spirit (realized it) you became the spirit. You saw Christ you became Christ. You saw the father, you shall become the father.**

You "saw the spirit" within you and realized it was you. You realized who Christ is, and you became one with him. You see what God is, and you will realize you are of the same consciousness. Your individual form is like a cell in the body of God. But you are not the cell; you are that which is life itself within you and around you. This quest to "know thy self" serves as the central theme in all these gospels, and self-knowledge serves as the vehicle for entering the kingdom. In the Gospel of Philip Jesus goes on to explain:

> **It is not necessary for all those who possess everything to know themselves? Some indeed, if they do not know themselves, they will not enjoy what they possess. But those who have come to know themselves will enjoy their possessions.**

Ignorance is the cause of suffering on earth. The Kabbalah teaches us that man's fall from grace was due to his ignorance, in that he (Adam) ignored God and his loving advice, and that causes his suffering. Our separation from God is what causes pain since God is life itself. When we ignore or deny God's presence in our life, we suffer. Our mental desires and selfishness are what separate us from our Creator and the loving guidance given by our Creator. This loving guidance is the apple on the Tree of Life. Whereas, the Tree of Knowledge bears the apple of the ego, selfishness, and desires. When we realize the living presence of God within us and are, therefore, no longer living in ignorance of that divine presence, which is guiding us, we are not inclined to sin. We find happiness and peace at God's side right here on earth. Christ makes it even clearer for us:

> Ignorance is the mother of all evil. Ignorance will result in death, because those that come from ignorance neither were, nor are, nor shall be perfect when all the truth is revealed.

So we are clearly being guided to inquire, to question, and to look within ourselves to find God. Jesus is guiding us to realize our own true spiritual nature and be fulfilled. Jesus takes it a step further to clarify this point in the following paragraph:

> If you know the truth, the truth will make you free. Ignorance is a slave. Knowledge is freedom. If we know the truth, we shall find the fruits of the truth within us. If we are joined to it, it will bring our fulfillment.

Thus, we see that Christ's closest apostles—Thomas, James, and Philip — all had gospels, written in the first and second centuries, long before the *New Testament* was created, that were read widely by Christians for generations. These early scriptures were not about accounts of Jesus' life, but directions and instructions on how to become enlightened. The original followers of Christ were studying the way to enlightenment by looking within to find God and realizing the kingdom of heaven that lies within them. These are universal teachings; they are the eternal truths that enlightened masters from around the world have been teaching for many ages, but look at how eloquent and powerful Christ's explanations are.

One of the most important of all Jesus' disciples is Mary Magdalene. She is well known as one of Christ's closest disciples in the New Testament, but when we read the apostle's Canon we see that she plays an even bigger role than we would assume from reading only the New Testament. Mary is given not only special attention but special information about the mysteries of the universe that Jesus only teaches her. She is also sent by Christ to relay messages to the other apostles, and she gives them instruction and shares with the disciples what she has learned in private from Jesus. Mary becomes an apostle to the apostles.

Mary Magdalene

Mary Magdalene was one of Christ's closest disciples. Sometimes Mary is referred to as Mary Magdala, as she was believed to have been from the Galilean town of Magdala. Mary plays an important role in Christ's story. The New Testament recounts that Mary accompanied Jesus on his last journey to Jerusalem (Mark 15:41); she was with Christ during his crucifixion (Mark 15:33-40; Matthew 27:45-55; *Luke* 224-49; John 19: 25-30); and she was the first among the apostles to witness the resurrection of Christ (although she did not recognize him at first) and tells the other apostles (John 20:1-2). However, in the apostle's canon and in earlier Christian writings she plays an even more important role. In the Gospel of Philip, Mary is referred to as Jesus' "companion," and in the Gospel of Mary she is acknowledged as a leader among the disciples.

Mary Magdalene is sometimes portrayed as a **prostitute** or adulteress, but the New Testament does not say so and neither does the apostle's canon. Luke writes that Jesus casts seven demons from her, and afterward she joined the movement and became a disciple. In a sermon, Pope Gregory (in the fourth century) identifies Mary as *peccatrix*, a sinful woman, using her as a model for the repentant sinner, but he never calls her a prostitute. However in later centuries she is associated with the adulteress recounted in John 8, and the church fathers' considered her sin being unchaste. The Eastern Orthodox Church distinguishes Mary Magdalene from the sinful woman portrayed in John and strongly denies that she was ever a prostitute. Mary is the first to anoint Christ with oil signifying that he is the long awaited Messiah, and as we shall see, she is also considered the disciple closest to Jesus.

The Gospel of Mary

The Gospel of Mary is believed to have been written in the first century and is also a part of the Nag Hammadi Library discovered in Egypt; other fragments of this gospel have been found that date to the middle of the first to second century, including: Papyrus Berollnensis, Papyrus Oxyrhynchus, Papyrus Rylands as well as the Berlin Codex. So we know this gospel is among the very first gospels ever written.

It was read by many groups of Christians throughout the Holy Land in the first and second centuries by the original Jewish Christians in the Holy Land. According to Karen L. King, Winn Professor of Ecclesiastical History at Harvard University in the Divinity School, in her book *The Gospel of Mary, Jesus and the First Woman Apostle* the Gospel of Mary teaches us that: "Salvation is achieved by discovering within oneself the true spiritual nature of humanity and overcoming the deceptive entrapments of the bodily passions and the world." According to Professor King, Jesus is teaching the disciples not to follow "some heroic leader or a set of rules and laws" but, rather, to "seek the child of true Humanity within themselves and gain inward peace."

The Gospel of Mary can be divided into two sections: the first describes a dialog between the risen Christ and his disciples and the second contains a description of a conversation Jesus has with Mary and her conveyance of his message to the other apostles. Mary is rich with deep philosophical ideas and explanations; here Jesus reveals the nature of existence, sin, and our own eternal nature. The first few lines from the text are missing and the first words we hear Jesus speaking to the disciples are:

> All natures, all formations, all creatures exist in and with one another, and they will be resolved again into their own roots. For the nature of matter is resolved into the roots of its nature alone. He who has ears to hear, let them hear.

All creatures exist in and with each other as spirit. The roots of matter lie in that which provides for their existence, which is the life force within them, that is them. Here again we hear Jesus explaining our own intrinsic higher nature and inspiring us to go within and discover it. Then Peter asks the Lord, "Since you have explained everything to us, tell us this also: What is the sin of the world?" The Savior said:

> **There is no sin, but it is you who make sin when you do things that are like the nature of adultery, which is called "sin." That is why the Good came into your midst, to the essence of every nature, in order to restore it to its root.**

We learn two important precepts from this answer from Christ: First, that there is no "original sin." Sin is not something that was carried down to you from ancient man and woman, Adam and Eve, for which you need to be forgiven, but it is what you do when you know better—when you go unconscious. Moreover, Jesus points out that there is good in our nature, and that we are to go within and find it and bring it out. This is a Kabalistic concept that Jesus is explaining. There is a spark of divinity within each of us that is our own abiding nature, and our purpose is to become aware of or gain knowledge (gnosis) of this divine nature. As we come to know ourselves, our true divine nature can guide the lower nature of the mind and senses to right thoughts, words, and actions. Then Jesus said:

> **Peace be with you. Receive my peace to yourselves. Beware that no one lead you astray, saying, "Lo here!" or "Lo there!" For the Son of Man is within you. Follow after him! Those who seek him will find him. Go then and preach the gospel of the kingdom. Do not lay down any rules beyond what I appointed for you, and do not give a law like the lawgiver lest you be constrained by it.**

Jesus is stating quite clearly to be leery of people who lead you to look outside of yourself for the answers for the Son of Man lies within us. He warns us of church authoritarianism. Further, he seems to be telling us not to make rules and create a dogma like those of the temple priests or church fathers, but, rather, to seek within to find the answers. It's not a belief; it's an experience. You don't achieve it through rituals or rites but through your own investigation, inquiry, and realization. We are not supposed to just blindly follower church leaders but to go within and to realize this truth for ourselves.

After Christ departs from them, the apostles are grieved at his leaving and Mary says to them "Do not weep and do not grieve nor be irresolute, for his grace will be entirely with you and protect you. But let us praise his greatness, for he has prepared us and made us into men." Here Mary is addressing the disciples as peers, providing loving guidance and direction. Then Peter says to Mary:

> Sister, we know that the Savior loved you more than the rest of women. Tell us the words of the Savior which you remember — which you know but we do not, nor have we heard them.

This section is most revealing, for it demonstrates that Jesus had imparted special knowledge to Mary and the apostles knew it. This was an age where women had a very low status in society, so for Jesus to impart special knowledge indicates his respect for her. The fact that the disciples would ask her for this information shows that they knew Jesus respects her and thinks her worthy. So now the disciples are looking to Mary to gain additional insights. Mary answered and said:

> What is hidden from you I will proclaim to you…I saw the Lord in a vision and I said to him, "Lord, I saw you today in a vision.'… He answered and said to me, "Blessed are you, that you did not waver at the sight of me'…I said to him "Lord, now does he who sees the vision see it through the soul or through the spirit?" The Savior answered and said. "He does not see through the soul nor through the spirit, but the mind which is between the two."

All visions and all phenomena experienced through the senses are of the mind. Time, space, energy, and matter are of the mind, and they are temporal, fleeting, and ultimately unreal. Spirit is what underlies the expression of the divine in form. It is what animates our existence.

The soul is what the self identifies with and what holds the patterns through which spirit is expressed; the mind is the interface.

The Magdalene Papyrus

The Magdalene Papyrus. These three scraps, just a few square centimeters each from a codex with Greek writing on papyrus, were discovered in 1901 in Luxor, Egypt. The redating of these relics in 1994 with more precise scientific means indicated that these segments of the Gospel of Mary date to the first century, possibly as early as 60 CE. This makes them older than the second century fragments of John's Gospel at the John Ryland Library in Manchester that date to 125 CE, and are eight centimeters in height. Thus, the Gospel of Mary is one of the greatest discoveries in Christian history and is a historically more reliable source of information on what Jesus actually said. In this gospel we see Mary appears as an apostle to the apostles; Jesus gives her special knowledge and she even advises the other apostles. A whole church is created that aligns with Mary's teaching called the **Carpocrations,** who develop quite a large congregation throughout Israel. The Carpocrations have female bishops who give baptisms, but the Greco-Roman church disbanded the whole group because they were considered heretics.

So, although Mary is not listed in the New Testament as one of the original twelve apostles, she clearly becomes one of the leaders of the new church, and the apostles learn that Jesus respects her enough to share these higher teachings with her that even they don't know. Christ first comes to her after his Resurrection, and he asks her to tell the others that he has returned. She was the closest to Jesus, and her gospel was well known to Christians in the first century. But by the second century her role was being marginalized, her gospel was rejected, and women could no longer serve as bishops or baptize. Rome put an end to that.

To the first Christians in the Holy Land, Christ was not a god; he was a naturally born son of Joseph and Mary, a descendent of King David, and believed by his early followers to be the Messiah and an enlightened master. Of the eleven or so Christian scriptures from the Holy Land that date from the first to second centuries, there is no evidence that any of the original disciples believed that Jesus died for their sins or that they were redeemed by his Crucifixion. They don't accept Paul or his epistles either, and this is why these Jewish Christian gospels were deliberately omitted from the Greek New Testament. From these beginnings, the movement branched out into other lands and two groups of Christ's followers formed: the orthodoxy from the pagan Greek and Roman lands (primarily to the north) and the Gnostics who tended to dwell in the Holy Land (primarily to the south). In the next chapter we will look at Gnosticism and the following chapter the orthodoxy.

• • •

Gnosticism and Heresies

Gnosticism is the practice or study of gnosis, which is Greek for knowledge; more specifically used in the context of a spiritual awakening or enlightenment, as opposed to an intellectual understanding or rational deduction. *Agnostic* refers to one who lacks the awareness of God or does not believe God is knowable, whereas a Gnostic either has direct awareness of God or is seeking it. Forms of Gnosticism appear to have been developing in the years before Christ, with esoteric influences of the Greeks, Egyptians, Persians, Hindus, and Kabalistic Judaism all fostering a spiritual movement of self-awareness in the first century.

Gnosticism refers to a wide range of divergent groups, beliefs, and practices. There are Greek Gnostics that embrace parts of Platonic and neo-Platonic philosophies, the Kabbalists, and Jewish-Christian Gnostics, Sethian Gnostics, Valentinian Gnostics, as well as those aligned with, Hermetic teachings, Mithran cults and many other independent groups that all get clumped into the term Gnostic. As the Roman Church consolidated control over the independent churches, the term Gnostic became applied to any spiritual teaching that was not orthodox. Orthodox means *right way*, and those that did not agree with the bishops in Rome, or had beliefs or practices that differed from orthodox ones (theirs), were called heretics. A heretic was anyone who disagreed with the Orthodox or Roman Church, thus, over time the Gnostics, including the original Jewish Christian, all became heretics.

As we are primarily interested here in Jesus Christ's message, we will focus on the gnostic elements of the early Christian church, and draw distinctions among the other gnostic schools. As we move farther away in time from the apostolic age and closer to the Council of Nicea (325 CE) when the canon was created we see both the orthodox and the gnostic schools expand and embellish earlier teachings. In the two centuries before the council took place, many new gospels and stories were coming out about Jesus and those later accounts hold less authenticity amongst scholars. Nonetheless, although there was a concerted effort to stamp out these competing elements within the Church, they continued for centuries.

By the beginning of the second century, many new tales of Jesus' birth and childhood had been written, which we are going to discuss here, but first it is important to note that as we move away from the Jewish or Aramaic-speaking Christians, to those scriptures produced within the Hellenized culture, the tone, language, audience, and the message itself changes considerably, as these following examples indicate. None of the apostle's gospels have accounts of Jesus' Immaculate Conception or resurrection or is there any discussion of his death being for the remission of sin. The eleven books just mentioned in the preceding two chapters that were written earlier all tell a different tale of Jesus showing them the way to enlightenment, this shows up again and again consistently as the focus of his teaching. By the second century, cultures unfamiliar with Judaism or Aramaic writings were adapting the word to their own cultural paradigms and in so doing, they changed the core theology of Christ's teachings. According to George M. Lamsa in his book *Idioms in the Bible Explained and a Key to the Original Gospels*:

> In the second century A.D. the Jews saw that Pagan customs, Greek and Egyptian traditions and religious commercialism were creeping into Christianity. Doctrines and dogma were replacing the teachings of Jesus and those of the Prophets, and there was danger of Jewish amalgamation with Gentiles. Therefore the Jews dropped their interest, and took no more part in what was then known as a Gentile movement

As the Gentile church membership grows, these new groups only want to include Paul's work and eliminate any of the Jewish gospels, or any "Jewishness" from their Greek Bible. The first Bible ever compiled was Marcion's Bible, and Marcion only wanted Paul's writing and intentionally eliminated all Jewish mention. The entire Old Testament and all four of the New Testament gospels were removed from this Bible because they were deemed too Jewish. Marcion lived from 85-160 CE, so anti-Semitism was already growing strong by the beginning of the second century. By the second century, entirely new stories about Christ were being written and disseminated within both the Orthodox and within Gnostic Churches.

Christians had been persecuted by both Romans and Jews; the non-Jewish Christians began resenting Jews and became increasingly anti-Semitic. The fact that Jews would not accept Jesus as their Messiah incensed the bishops because it essentially suggests that the bishops were wrong. This anti-Semitism plays a large role in the development of the church canon and the development of Christianity, and shows at least part of the reason why the apostles' canon and the earliest Christian scriptures weren't included in the Greek New Testament. In excluding the Jewish Christian scriptures from the New Testament canon, the world almost lost Christ's Word. If the world's greatest historians and scholars tell us that these Jewish Christian gospels are authentic and were read by Christ's closest disciples, then why are we not all reading them? Something happened, and you need to know what happened each step of the way and why.

As you read these more Gnostic accounts from the next, second, and third, centuries note the change in language; everything becomes more embellished, and the stories start sounding more like Greek mythology than Jewish mysticism. These scriptures were clearly not written by actual witnesses of the gospel or by Jews because they reflect the changes in culture and writing style more indicative of the Greeks and Romans. None of these scriptures are considered authentic by either historians or the church, but they serve as excellent examples of how the way Christ was viewed was changing from one culture to another and from the first century to the second and third.

The Apostle Peter

The Apostle Peter is one of Christ's first apostles and a principal leader of the Jesus movement. Originally known as Simon, Peter is often addressed as Simon Peter or Cephas, which means *rock* as does the name Peter. Saint Peter was born in Bethsaida (John 1:44), the son of Jonah or John. Peter's mother-in-law was healed by Jesus at their home in Capernaum (Matthew 8:14-17). Peter (then called Simon) was a fisherman along with his brother Andrew, when Jesus calls upon them to be "fishers of men" (Matthew 4:18-19; Mark 1:16-17), and they join his ministry and become his first apostles. In Luke we learn that Simon (Peter) owns the boat that Jesus uses to preach to the multitudes who were pressing on him at the shore of Lake Gennesaret (Luke 5:3). Jesus then tells them to lower their nets, and they become amazed as fish filled their nets, and that miracle inspires them to follow Jesus (Luke 5:4-11).

Peter is always placed among the top of the leadership within the early church, but his role differs amongst the various branches of Christianity. After the Crucifixion, Peter undertook a missionary journey to Lydda, Joppa, and Caesarea (Acts 9:32-10:2), becoming one of the first apostles to evangelize to the Gentiles (Acts 10). Of the original twelve apostles, Peter was most supportive of Paul in revising the requirements for joining the movement as a Gentile. About half way through Acts the narrative switches from Peter to Paul, and we learn a little more about Peter's acts. The New Testament book of Galatians (2:11-14) mentions he was with Paul in Antioch, and tradition holds that he is the first patriarch of Antioch. According to Eastern tradition Peter had then traveled to Mesopotamia, founded churches there, and died in Babylon.

The New Testament does not tell us that Peter ever went to Rome, but the Roman tradition has it that he did. The Catholic Church maintains that Peter died in Rome, but that fact is not supported by the Gospel of Peter. The First Epistle of Peter ends with the reference "The church that is in Babylon, chosen together with you, salutes you, and so does my son, Mark" (1 Pet 5:13). The Catholic Church maintains that this reference to Babylon refers to Rome, and that makes Rome the center of the church and this created an apostolic succession down to the current pope. However, the Eastern Christians' account is that he, in fact, went to Babylon. This would make sense since he had ancestors there and spoke their tongue. The Orthodox Church recognizes Peter as one of the leaders of the church but does not consider him to have any princely role over his fellow apostles.

In the Gospel of Matthew, where Jesus says "You are Peter, and on this rock I will build my Church," the Orthodox Church holds that Christ is referring to the confession of faith not the person of Peter (whose name means rock). The word used here is in the feminine, suggesting the strength of faith like a rock, whereas, if Jesus were referring to Peter personally, he would have used the masculine. Lutherans and other Protestants refer to Ephesians 2:20, which states that the Church's foundation are the apostles and prophets, instead of Peter alone, and that Rome has no privilege over other ministries, "the same keys that are given to Peter in Matthew 16 are given to the whole church of believers in Matthew 18." Nonetheless, Peter's role is pivotal, and his contribution immeasurable.

The Apocalypse of Peter

The Apocalypse of Peter, also known as the Revelation of Peter, is indicative of the next generation of Christian writing that developed in the second century and serves as an example of apocalyptic Christian literature with Hellenistic overtones. It too is a treasure of the Nag Hammadi Library, but fragments of it have shown up at other sites too, such as Akhmin in Upper Egypt. We also learn of Peter's version of the Apocalypse from the church fathers who debated using it in place of Revelation in the New Testament. The **Muratorian** fragment, the earliest existing list of canonic writings of the New Testament (175-200 CE) includes the Apocalypse of Peter, and states "the Apocalypses also of John and Peter only do we receive, which some among us would read in church." Peter's revelation was widely read until the Council of Nicea, which eventually rejected it for being too Gnostic. Most historians believe that the Gospel of Peter was not written by Saint Peter himself but rather is an inspired writing attributed to him.

In the first chapter of the Revelation of Peter, moving forward to the second century now, Peter is telling us that he is asking the Lord:

> **Declare to us what are the signs of your coming and of the end of the world, that we may perceive and mark the time of your coming and instruct those who come after us, to whom we preach the word of your gospel, and whom we install in your church, that they, when they hear it, may take heed to themselves and mark the time of your coming.**

Now note, up to now, in the Jewish Christian Gospels we have not heard stories about "the signs of your coming." They were to look within to find him. Jesus makes that explicit. There was no discussion or warning of the end of the world; they were ending the world they knew through their mind and senses, and were awakening to a new higher awareness of God's living presence on earth. Now they fear the end, and in this story the Lord answered saying:

> Take heed that no one deceive you and that you be not doubters and serve other gods. Many shall come in my name saying, 'I am Christ.' Believe them not, neither draw near to them. For the coming of the Son of God shall not be plain; but as the lighting that shines from the east to the west, so will I come upon the clouds of heaven with a great host in my majesty; with my cross going before my face will I come in my majesty; shining seven times brighter than the sun will I come in my majesty with all my saints, my angels. And my father shall set a crown upon my head, that I may judge the quick and the dead and recompense every one according to his works.

Jesus called himself, and the apostles called him, the Son of Man, and now he's being introduced as the Son of God. Instead of joining Christ in a kingdom already "spread out upon the earth," he is coming out of the clouds like the gods **Zeus** or **Thor**, with lighting and thunder. That doesn't sound like any messiah of the Jews; the Jews were not anticipating the end of the world, but they were anticipating Zion. The Messiah was never thought of as a god, he was God's agent on earth. He was revered, respected, and awe inspiring but never a god himself. But in a world of human like gods and goddesses the pagan church began depicting Jesus as a god, or as the most popular savior in the Greco-Roman world at this time Apollonius of Tyana.

Notice how different the writing style is. By the second century Jesus was "seven times brighter than the sun," flying through space with a troupe of angels, and getting a "crown put upon his head." The Gospel of Peter also goes into a great deal of negativity; we hear "blasphemers are hung by the tongue." In the second century, we start hearing threats; we move from finding peace within to a focus on punishment, hell, and damnation. This gospel is very fear based, whereas the apostles' canon is very positive and affirming. Originally the emphasis of the way was not, apparently, on sin and redemption but on finding eternal happiness and peace within, and then creating this peace on earth. They were not waiting for a future coming or a second coming or an end of humanity, but, rather, they were looking for a realization of God through Christ right here and now, as we are witnessing today. Scholars believe this work is pseudepigraphic, that is, attributed to Peter by later writers within a pagan culture sometime in the second century.

The Gospel of Peter is more Greek than Hebrew, and it is clear that the writer of the Gospel of Peter's views, are more aligned with Paul's view of Christ "speaking from the Clouds," than those of James, Thomas, Philip or Mary or with the Gospels of the Ebionites, the Nazarenes, the Hebrews or Egyptians. By the second century, Jesus began to take on the attributes of the Greek gods and the Persian god-man Mithra. Jesus Christ became the all encompassing deity of the Greco-Roman pagan world. The Jesus movement spawns new ideas and perspectives that are evolving and changing, and we can follow these changes through both the Gnostic and Pauline schools of thought through the second and third centuries.

Gnostic Proliferation

Into the cultural milieu of Gnosticism, along with the heavy Greek influences, were those of other neighboring lands. The Persian Schools of Gnosticism are amongst the oldest, originating in western Persia in the province of Babylon (Bagdad) around the second century. There were two primary schools of thought in Persia: Mandaeanism and Manichaeism. **Mandaeanianism** is still practiced in the southern Iraq and the Iranian province of Khuzestan. The word Mandaean comes from *Manda d-Heyyi*, which means knowledge of life. They revere John the Baptist and have a book of John the Baptist called *Sidra d-iahia*. Their primary religious scripture is called the Genza Rabba. Although they have close ties with early Christianity, their practice is more of an internal spiritual practice than a religion per se. They respect but do not follow Moses, Jesus, or Mohammed, and they use the right of baptism as a ritual of internal cleansing similar to the Essenes. **Manichaeism** was founded by the prophet Mani (210-276 CE) who taught that "The true God has nothing to do with the material world or cosmos." They believed that the Jews, Christians, and Pagans were worshiping a false God of their own creation.

Another rather broad area of Gnosticism is **Syrian-Egyptian Gnosticism**. It is heavily influenced by Platonist (Plato's) theology but also blends in elements of the Torah, Kaballah, and the indigenous cultural elements from each respective province or country where it is practiced. It typically depicts creation as coming from a series of emanations from a primal monadic source. In these schools, evil is seen as a part of the material world, whereas, good comes from another plane or heaven. Evil is viewed as a lack of insight, or realization, of our true divine nature. In these Gnostic schools, salvation comes through gnosis, a realization that comes from within, as taught by Jesus Christ. This body of Christianity was very large in the second century, and some historians believe it was the largest before the Pauline school of theology gained the majority by the third century.

Many of these gnostic concepts are remarkably similar to certain Hindu and Buddhist teachings. Early third- and fourth-century writers Hippolytus and Epiphanius write about Scythianus who had visited India around 50 CE and brought back what they call "the Doctrine of the Two Principles." According to Cyril of Jerusalem, Scythianus' pupil Terebinthus referred to himself as being a Buddhist and states that "He called himself a Buddas." Ultimately Terebinthus settled in Babylon, where he is believed to have transmitted his teachings to Mani, who then founded Manichaeism. So Buddhism apparently also had an influence on Christian theology as well. Quoting the church father Cyril of Jerusalem (Catechetical lecture 6):

> But Terebinthus, his disciple in this wicked error, inherited his money and books and heresy, and came to Palestine, and becoming known and condemned in Judaea he resolved to pass into Persia; but lest he should be recognized there also by his name he changed it and called himself Buddas.

The third-century Syrian writer and Christian Gnostic Bar Daisan describes how holy men from India frequently came to the Holy Land. As mentioned in the preceding chapter, Jews had begun settling along the Malabar Coast of southwest India and had established trade relations with Jews from the Holy Land. So, information and ideas had been passing through the Holy Land from India for centuries. Moreover, as mentioned in chapter three in the discussion of the axial age, many of the metaphors Jesus uses, such as, the blind leading the blind and the mustard seed were well established in the Hindu writing called the Upanisads. The yogi seeks to find the kingdom of heaven that lies within, this is the path to enlightenment, and when one enlightens he becomes one with the father of creation. These concepts run throughout the Vedas, the Upanisads and the Hindu epics.

In Gnostic texts we see cosmologies that are both dualistic and monistic. In dualistic Gnosticism, we see forces of good and evil fighting it out. Here we are trapped in a state of darkness and ignorance, dulled through our own mind and senses, but through self-awareness we transcend those passions of the mind and become enlightened. Monism views God as a greater interconnected whole, without semi divine counterparts or a plurality of metaphysical deities.

There are two principal schools of second-century Christian Gnosticism: Sethian and Valentinian. Sethian schools tend to be more dualistic and Valentinian schools are more monistic. In her book *The Gnostic Gospels*, Elaine Pagels states that "Valentinian Gnosticism… differs essentially from dualism," and in *Gnostic Monism and the Gospel of Truth* William Schoedel states that "a standard element in the interpretation of Valentinianism and similar forms of Gnosticism is the recognition that they are fundamentally monistic." So the Sethians are transcending evil to realize God, and the Valentinians are realizing the transcendental presence of God within, but they both seek salvation through the gnosis given by Jesus the Christ.

In reading Gnostic texts it is important to realize that the authors are speaking to us in metaphor. We are not intended to take the symbolism literally. They are trying to explain the unexplainable and use names for God and his attributes, various emanations of the divine, and states of consciousness to represent aspects of their theology. The Old Testament, the New Testament and the Gnostic Testaments all need to be read as mythologies that impart deeper meanings to get the gist of their wisdom at a deeper level. Literal translations of Gnostic scripture only address the precepts superficially. When you read deeper into the symbolism and look for the underlying messages, a whole new depth of perception is revealed. The names sound strange because we attempt to translate figurative meaning with literal ones or don't understand the cognitive associations being made with these names, and they are all translated from other languages. The following provides an overview of some basic Sethian concepts.

Sethian Gnosticism

Sethian refers to Seth, the third son of Adam and Eve (after Cain and Abel), who is believed to be the possessor and disseminator of gnosis. He is often related to Jesus, serving a similar role in saving humanity from evil. Sethian works include the Apocryphon of John, the Apocalypse of Adam, The Three-fold First Thought, The Holy Book of the Great Invisible Spirit, Allogenes (Foreigner) and the Three Steles of Seth, among others. Sethian revelations tend to be quite cosmological. Sethian texts often refer to various emanations of God called *Aeons*. God is beyond form and may be referred to as the Aion teleos (the perfect Aeon), the One, the Monad, Bythos (meaning Depth or Profundity), Proarkhe (Before the Beginning) or just E Arkhe (the Beginning). This first being also has an inner being or quality, within itself called either Ennoia (thought), Charis (grace), or Sige (silence). The "split perfect being" further conceives a second Aeon Caen (power) and a feminine power Akhana (truth, love). These Aeons typically come in pairs, and together they constitute what is called the *pleroma* or region of light. Of course, the lowest region of the pleroma is the physical world to which we are here to bring the light. These ideas and attributes of the divine are also reflected in the Kabbalah and relate to the ascension of consciousness described in the *Sefer Yetzirah* known as the Tree of Life, described in chapter three.

Read the following passage as a metaphor, understanding that each name represents an attribute or expression of the divine. When an

Aeon named Sophia (mind) emanated without her partner aeon, the result was the Demiurge, or half-creator, sometimes called *Yaldabaoth*, that plagues mankind and keeps us in darkness. In other words, coming into form without full consciousness is hell. Because there was an outer manifestation without a corresponding inner light, Jesus and the Holy Spirit had come to earth to bring balance back to the universe. Similar to how in George Lukas's **Star Wars** mythology, Skywalker is believed to be the one who will bring balance back to The Force of the universe, Jesus has come to bring balance back to earth, which is being ruled by the dark side in the view of Sethian Christian Gnosticism.

Christ incarnates on earth as the man Jesus to be able to teach man how to achieve gnosis and return to his heavenly abode or state. The Demiurge refers to an entity typically depicted as evil, who is responsible for creating this physical and spiritually unaware world—the world of illusion that is represented by the devil. There is a divine presence that is transcendental to the Creator God of the Old Testament, and Jesus has come to take us there. In this Gnostic paradigm Sophia's power has become enclosed within the material forms of humanity; we have fallen asleep and are blinded by and to the light within us that is our own true nature. The objective of this Sethian Gnosticism is to awaken this spark of divinity and live in the true state of God realization.

The Secret Book of John

The Secret Book of John or **Aprocryphon of John** is a classic second-century Sethian Gnostic text written sometime before 180 CE that is filled with beautiful metaphors. Here Jesus Christ reappears after his Ascension to give secret knowledge (gnosis) to the disciple John, the son of Zebedee. This book contains one of the clearest expositions of the Gnostic myths of creation and redemption, and explains the existence of evil in the world. In one mythology Yaltabaoth (the demiurge or creator of the lower physical world) is tricked into breathing the breath of life into the humans he has made, thus imparting the divine power of Sophia (divine wisdom) into them. They become animate human beings but don't realize their own divine nature. Jesus then comes to impart the wisdom that will free them from the illusion or dream of their physical existence. The Apocalypes begins:

> **The teaching of the Savior, and the revelation of the mysteries, and the things hidden in silence**

The story goes on to explain how after John was chastised by a Pharisee named Arimanius at the temple in Jerusalem, he goes off into the desert to meditate. Upon sitting in his solitude, he has a vision:

> **Straightway, while I was contemplating these things, behold, the heavens opened and the whole of creation which is below heaven shone, and the world was shaken.**

John sees Jesus in multiple forms simultaneously and is initially scared by the vision, but Christ comforts him and begins to impart the knowledge of the race of the perfect man. Here we see the Jewish influence of a race of people who live righteously in accordance with God's law—God's chosen people. Jesus explains to John the nature of God:

> **The Monad is a monarchy with nothing above it. It is He who exists as God and Father of everything, the Invisible One who is above everything who exists as incorruption, which is in the pure light into which no eye can look.**

This description is similar to the Hindu concept of there being total potentiality or consciousness: Shiva, from which the godhead, divine being or universal intelligence is manifest; Vishnu, who dreams of the physically manifest universe; and Brahman the physically manifest universe. There is what of God we can see physically, there is a higher reality that is unseen, and there is the unfathomable and inconceivable reality. In trying to explain this to John in his vision, Jesus further describes the unknowable as:

> He is the invisible Spirit of whom it is not right to think of him as a God, or something similar. For he is more than a god, since there is nothing above him, for no one lords it over him.

The story goes on to describe the seven powers and 365 angels, and overcoming passions of the mind and vices to attain the superior awareness of God's living presence within us. These all allude to the symbolism of the Kabbalah, with its seven powers, names with power, angelic powers, and spark of divinity within us. As these concepts were absorbed by Greek culture and language, they also began to sound more Greek. Here we also see further development of eternal punishment, which had not previously been a part of the Christ's or the apostles' teachings. After John asks Christ where those souls go that do not transcend, the Lord replies:

> To that place where there is no repentance. And they will be kept for the day on which those who have blasphemed the spirit will be tortured, and they will be punished and eternal punishment..."

As we move deeper into the second and third centuries of Christian history, we see certain themes developing that appear to be influenced by Greek mythology, and the voice of Christianity becomes more Greek and then Roman. Throughout the second century many new Gnostic scriptures were being circulated that mention blasphemers and the various forms of punishment that we have no record of in the first century. Christianity is now taking on a sterner tone and becomes more fear based, authoritarian, and more Roman. There was no single clear and consistent doctrine for the church; each church had its own tradition and doctrines. Those in the north read more along the lines of Greek and Roman literature, those in the south were more Kabalistic and Hermetic, and still others picked up the character of the culture and mythologies of their region, such as, the Egyptian cult of Abraxas.

We also see an emphasis on sin, hell, and redemption that was not present in the earlier writings. The new focus is on judgment day and Christ's Second Coming. In contrast, early Jewish followers of Jesus were seeking him within to commune with him in the present moment. The new Christians, as they were starting to be called by the Greeks and Romans, were awaiting him to come again…one day. A myriad of stories started to be created about the when, where, why, and hows of this Second Coming and of the end of days that relate to Greek mythology.

In another second-century codex from Nag Hammadi called the **First Thought in Three Forms**, also called the Trimorphic Protennoia, we begin to see the development of God's character and expression as having three forms. The divine is depicted as the first thought (*Protennoia*) that reveals her greatness (feminine energy) through her descent and manifestation into the physical realm in three different forms (the triple power). In his *Lost Scriptures*, Bart D. Ehrman explains these descents and attributes as follows:

> [S]he is Thought of the Father (or Voice), the Mother (or Sound), and the Son (or Word, i.e., the Logos). It is her final descent in the appearance of human flesh that brings the ultimate illumination to those who dwell in ignorance and darkness, leading to their ascent into the world of Light.

Second-century Gnostic literature makes use of the feminine to depict the spirit. Here we also see one of the first attempts to describe what later became known as the Trinity—God the Father, Son, and Holy Ghost. You also can see how the spirit is presented in the feminine, similar to how the Kabbalists refer to the Sekinah. In *The Gnostic Gospels*, Elaine Pagels states: "one striking difference between these 'heretical' sources and orthodox ones: Gnostic sources continually use sexual symbolism to describe God." The Sethian Gnostics are looking to make union with God and become enlightened. In another Sethian Christian Gnostic codex called **Allogenes** (The Stranger), an initiate called Messos receives a vision of a feminine power called Youel who tells him:

> Since your instruction has become complete, and you have known the good that is within you, hear concerning the Triple Power those things that you will guard in great silence and mystery.

Then Allogenes pronounces the enlightenment of the consciousness:

> I was very disturbed, and I turned to myself...Having seen the light that surrounded me and the good that was within me, I became divine.

The Gospel of Judas Iscariot

One of the most fascinating of the new discoveries is the Gospel of Judas Iscariot, one of Jesus' original twelve apostles, and the one who was entrusted with the money. But he is best known for his betrayal of Christ, selling out to the Jews and Romans for thirty pieces of silver. He lead Roman soldiers to the place where he knew Jesus would be and identified him by greeting him with a kiss, the Judas kiss. Afterward Judas kills himself, but the New Testament contradicts itself as to how. In the Gospel of Matthew it says that the guilt-ridden Judas returned the bribe to the priests and committed suicide by hanging himself. The Acts of the Apostles says he used the bribe to buy a field, but he fell down and "burst asunder in the midst, and all his bowels gushed out." This field is called Akeldama, or the field of blood. So, even in the New Testament we see how Matthew, the Jewish account, is more straightforward and objective, and Acts, the Greek scripture, which was written later, embellishes the account as if it were a Greek tragedy with "bowels gushed out" and "bursting asunder."

In the 1970s a leather-bound Coptic papyrus called The Gospel of Judas was discovered near Ben Masah, Egypt, and has been carbon dated to between the third and fourth centuries. This gospel was likely written late in the second century and is also a Sethian Christian Gnostic text that was known to Irenaeus and cited in his *Against Heresies* written around 180 CE. Through this interpretation of Christ's arrest, Judas acted out a role that was his destiny; the author maintains that Judas did what he did so that mankind might be redeemed by the death of Jesus' mortal body. Jesus expects him to go through with it in order for the prophesy to be fulfilled. In the canonical Gospel of John (13:27), it states what Jesus says to Judas as he is leaving the last supper to get the Romans: "Do quickly what you have to do." In other words, Jesus knew he was going to be betrayed by Judas, and he was actually working with Judas to make sure that it would happen; Jesus could have left since he was aware of the impending betrayal, but he let it happen.

In the Gospel of Judas Jesus explains to Judas what he must do, and what the consequences and rewards are for such devotion:

> "You shall be cursed for generations" and then "You will come to rule over them", and then "You will exceed all of them, for you will sacrifice the man that clothes me."

There is a fascinating account in this gospel of Jesus speaking with his disciples, and they clearly are not receiving his message. They sit down to offer prayer of thanksgiving over bread, and Jesus laughs at them. They, of course, are perplexed at his behavior and ask him why he is laughing. He explains that he is not laughing at them, but pointing out how they are just following rituals; in other words, why are you going out there to find God when he is right here. He says to them:

> I am not laughing at you. You are not doing this because of your own will but because it is through this that your god will be praised.

Then Jesus says to them "How do you know me? Truly I say to you, no generation of the people that are among you will know me." Apparently, the disciples are not quite getting it, and they become sad. Judas was the only one to speak up and said to Jesus:"I know who you are and where you have come from. You are from the immortal realm of Barbelo (beyond the beyond). And I am not worthy to utter the name of the one who has sent you." Then Jesus has a private conversation with Judas "knowing that Judas was reflecting upon something that was exalted", saying:

> **Step away from the others and I shall tell you the mysteries of the Kingdom. It is possible for you to reach it, but you will grieve a great deal. For someone else will replace you, in order that the twelve disciples may again come to completion with their god.**

The Infancy Gospels

During the second century a number of new books were being circulated about Jesus' birth, childhood, and the miracles that he performed. These books are believed by scholars and the church to demonstrate a lack of understanding of Jewish traditions and are not considered historically accurate or canonical but served as popular reading in its day. Many of these stories are also told in the Koran, the holy book of Islam, which reveres Jesus as a prophet of God.

The Infancy Gospel of James, also known as the Protoevangelium (before Christ's ministry) of James, may be the earliest surviving document attesting to the veneration of Mary by stating her perpetual virginity (19-20) and presenting her as the new Eve (13). Earlier, Jewish Christians believed that Mary and Joseph conceived Jeshua together as the Davidic heir, as Jewish prophesy declares. Moreover, Mary's perpetual virginity would not be in keeping with Abraham's covenant with God to populate Israel with "as many of his people as there are stars in the sky." Perpetual virginity and immaculate conceptions are not a part of the Hebrew tradition, but they are a part of Greek tradition, as we will discuss in the next chapter. This book goes so far as to have a midwife, who some think is Salome, perform a postpartum inspection of Mary to be assured of her virginity. This gospel also explains how James is actually the step-brother of Jesus, and that Joseph had James through a previous marriage. So this whole gospel, written over a century after Christ, was created to attempt to explain the unanswered questions posed when the Greco-Roman church embellished their stories and created these new mythologies about Jesus.

The Infancy Gospel of Thomas was another popular book that began circulating in the second century. The narrative begins with Jesus as a five-year-old boy and takes us to his twelfth year, when he would become a man. Here Jesus is depicted as a mischievous child who sometimes misuses his divine powers but learns to use them for good in the end. Here Jesus heals people, kills people, and brings people back to life. He confronts and challenges his teachers and helps his father in the workshop with his carpentry (stretching a board when needed). One of the favorite stories involves Jesus playing by the ford of a stream (2):

> [A]nd he gathered the flowing waters into pools and made them immediately pure. These things he ordered simply by speaking a word. He then made some soft mud and fashioned twelve sparrows from it. It was the Sabbath when he did this. A number of other children were also playing with him. But when a certain Jew saw what Jesus had done while playing on the Sabbath, he left right away and reported to his father. Joseph, 'Look, your child at the stream has taken mud and formed twelve sparrows. He has profaned the Sabbath.

Joseph then comes out to see what is happening, and he cries out to Jesus:

> "Why are you doing what is forbidden on the Sabbath." But Jesus clapped his hands and cries to the sparrows, "Be gone!" And the sparrows took flight and went off, chirping. When the Jews saw this they were amazed; and they went away and reported to their leaders what they had seen Jesus do.

This Greek writer misinterprets the Sabbath and is suggesting that Jesus does not have to live by Jewish law, another clear example of how the Greco-Roman church was distancing itself from Judaism. As you read these Gnostic texts, you note that as you move further along in time the stories of Jesus' miracles get bigger, Mary becomes a virgin, and even her mother, Anna, immaculately conceived Mary. Angels start appearing in these stories, Satan is talked about quite a bit, and there are many scary stories about hell. Jews start being depicted as evil and ignorant, and the new Greek-Roman leaders of the church presume to know better the teachings of Christ than those bishops from the Holy Land. Anti-Semitism is growing, and the Greco-Roman church leaders want to remove themselves of anything Jewish.

As the north begins to foreshadow the south, a whole new image of Jesus develops. Jesus goes from being a dark man to a white man. If you go to Egypt, you see depictions of the Hebrew slaves, among the Egyptians and other slaves from Africa. The Hebrews have darker skin than the Egyptians (who are light brown), but the Israelites are not as black as the African slaves. The Hebrews had long black hair and more prominent facial features, but the new church started painting Jesus with a white face, blond or light brown hair, and giving him the facial structure of a European man rather than a Hebrew. Jesus Christ was a man of color; he would have had Semite physical features and characteristics—dark skin and black hair. The church deliberately reconstructed him so he doesn't look or act like a Jew. He doesn't sound like a Jew either; he sounds like a Greek or Roman god thundering from the heavens. In the second century Jesus is completely remade into a Greco-Roman god. But there were church fathers in the south who kept the inner teaching alive, and one of the earliest and best known is Valentinius.

Valentinianism

Valentinius (100-160 CE) was the best known and initially most successful of the early Christian theologians. He and **Basilides,** another famous Gnostic leader, grew large congregations in Alexandria, Egypt, preaching the Gospel of Truth and how to become enlightened through Jesus Christ. Their more metaphysical form of Christianity is referred to as Valentnianism. Valentinius was born in Phrebonis in the Nile Delta, and he was educated in Alexandria, which was a major Christian center at the time and home to the greatest library and repository of spiritual information in the world. His Alexandrian followers said that Valentinius was a follower of Theudas, who studied under Paul of Tarsus (Saint Paul). He said that Paul had given Theudas secret wisdom that was in turn imparted to him to share with them.

After establishing a following in Alexandria, Valentinius went to Rome around 136 CE, during the pontificate of Pope Hyginus and remained until the pontificate of Pope Anicetus. While there **Valentinus** was almost made bishop (many believe of Rome), but in the end he was passed over and, according to tradition, went to Cyprus to teach. So, at one point in the early history of the church the Gnostic philosophy almost became orthodox. The church historian and critic Tertullian quotes in his *Adversus Valentinianos*:

> **Valentinius had expected to become a bishop, because he was an able man both in genius and eloquence. Being indignant, however, that another obtained the dignity by reason of a claim which confessorship had given him, he broke with the church of the true faith.**

The southern schools in Israel and Egypt were much more Gnostic, whereas the northern schools in the Greco-Roman culture were more Greco-Roman or pagan. There were those who were seeking Christ within in Israel, Syria, and Egypt, and those anticipating he was coming again any day, with war and destruction of the earth to all but a select few in Italy, Greece, and Turkey.

Basilides was the other great Alexandrian leader and father of the church, and a contemporary of Valentinius. He wrote twenty-four books on the gospel but all were destroyed by the Roman church years later. He was believed to be the pupil of the interpreter for Saint Paul, a man named Glaucias. Basilides taught during the reign of Hadrian (117-138), and what we know of what he taught was that God's mind (*nous*) or consciousness descended upon Jesus "as the dove at the Jordan." They believed that the Spirit of God is the redeemer not the crucified one. The body of Jesus was just the instrument of God, and the true Christ never died. There is an evolution or development of consciousness that brings us closer to the light until we realize that we are the light.

Although the works of Valentinius and Basilides were destroyed during the Gnostic purges of the Roman church, archeologists have recently discovered a codex from the Nag Hammadi Library that is known to be Valentinian, if not written by Valentinius himself. Two copies of this text have been found and were estimated to be written in Greek between 140 and 180 CE. Later Valentinius was declared a heretic and the church father of the next century, Irenaeus, ventures the following opinion:

> But the followers of Valentinius, putting away all fear, bring forward their own compositions and boast that they have more Gospels than really exist. Indeed their audacity has gone so far that they entitle their recent composition the Gospel of Truth.

The Gospel of Truth

The Gospel of Truth provides one of the clearest explanations of how to gain enlightenment through Jesus Christ. It is through this banned gospel that we first hear of the Trinity: the divine expressing through the Father, Son, and Holy Spirit. This is the first time this idea is proposed, and it is later adopted, but its origins are Gnostic. Here the Kabalistic notion of awakening the divine within us is also adopted and explained. In the fourth century, church father **Marcellus of Ancyra** declared that the idea of the godhead existed as three hypostases (hidden spiritual realities) and that idea came through Plato to Valentinius, according to Marcellus:

> Now the heresy of the Ariomanics, which has corrupted the Church of God...These then teach three hypostases, just as Valentinius the heresiarch first invented in the book entitled by him 'On the Three Natures.' For he was the first to invest three hypostases and three persons of the *Father, Son and Holy Spirit*, and he is discovered to have filched this from Hermes and Plato.

From a fragment of a letter written by Valentinius he writes "One [alone] is Good, whose free utterance is His manifestation through his Son; it is by Him alone that the heart can become pure." The material physical world is impure, there is darkness, and Christ has come to bring the light... to enlighten us. Valentinius is all about divine love, like a Sufi poet he has become intoxicated with divine love. Valentinius goes on to say:

> As far as I can see, the heart seems to receive somewhat the same treatment as an inn, which has holes and gaps made in its walls, and is frequently filled with dung, men living filthily in it and taking no care of the place as being someone else's property. Thus it is with the heart so long as it has no care taken of it, ever unclean and the abode of many daemons. But when the Alone Good Father hath regard unto it, it is sanctified and shineth with light; and he who possesseth such a heart, is so blessed that "he shall see God."

The Gospel of Truth is about the joy of enlightenment. God is love, and the reality is bliss. Here the gospel or good news is of God's revelation of gnosis or enlightenment, which comes through Jesus Christ. In Bart D. Ehrman's translation and commentaries on The Gospel of Truth in his book *Lost Scriptures*, he states:

> The book focuses on the truth that brings redemption to an anguished humanity languishing in darkness and ignorance, and especially on the one who brought this revealed truth, Jesus Christ, the Word who comes forth from the Father as his Son. Through Christ's revelation, the fog of error has been dissipated and the illusions of falsehood have been exposed, opening those who receive the truth to understand who they are, allowing them to be reunited with the incomprehensible and inconceivable Father of all.

What becomes clear in comparing first- and second-century writings to third- and fourth-century expositions is that the earlier ones indicate that their connection with Christ, and joining him in a heavenly state on earth, occurred whenever you received the word or became enlightened. As we move into later centuries, we see emphasis on him coming at some time in the future. But the Valentinians were seeking enlightenment now and the Gospel of Truth make this very clear. In the opening section of this gospel we are provided an exposition of man's fall from grace:

> Ignorance of the Father brought about anguish and terror; and the anguish grew solid like a fog, so that no one was able to see, for this reason error became powerful; it worked on its own matter foolishly, not having known the truth. It set about with a creation, preparing with power and beauty the substitute for the truth.

The Gnostic Gospel of Truth reads like the Upanishads of India, Vedantic philosophy, or Buddhist teachings with an *awakening of consciousness* as if from a slumber into a reality that is blissful and light: moksha, samadhi, or nirvana. These teachings echo the eternal truths propounded by the world's enlightened teachers, which validates those teachings rather than competes with them. All enlightened masters have recognized Jesus as an enlightened master, and even an avatar or incarnation of God in human form. They just don't believe he was the only one. Gnostics believe that we are all part of an interconnected whole, and this undifferentiated whole is described in the gospel as follows:

> As in the case of the ignorance of a person, when he comes to have knowledge, his ignorance vanishes of itself, as the darkness vanishes when light appears, so also the deficiency vanishes in the perfection. So from that moment on the form is not apparent, but it will vanish in the fusion of Unity, for now their works lie scattered. In time Unity will perfect the spaces. It is within Unity that each one will attain himself; within knowledge he will purify himself from multiplicity into Unity, consuming matter within himself like the fire, and darkness by light, death by life.

Awareness dispels ignorance as candlelight dispels darkness. This enlightenment of consciousness occurs (or appears to occur in the mind) when the individual consciousness is merged or liberated, and joins with the consciousness itself without being differentiated through the mind and senses. As all pain and suffering are caused through thinking or feeling one way or the other (like watching a play in our head), when we become ignorant of the divine presence within us and around us, it hurts. The more aware of God we are, the happier we are. So transcending these lower states of consciousness (guilt, shame, unworthiness, sadness, fear, anger, pride, etc) brings us into the kingdom of God and its blissful reality. It is universally described as being like awakening from a dream of unknowing. In the Gospel of Truth, this awakening of consciousness or gnosis is described as follows:

> Such is the way of those who have cast ignorance aside from them like sleep, not esteeming it as anything, nor do they esteem its works as solid things either, but they leave them behind like a dream in the night. The knowledge of the Father they value as the dawn. This is the way he has come to knowledge as if he had awakened. Good for the one who will return and awaken.

Over the millennium, thousands of people have attained these higher states of consciousness and have enlightened. Those that have not attained self-realization and have not found this bliss tend to discount it out of pride or ignorance. Others try to write it off as something neurological or as the result of fasting or something induced through drugs, deprivation of the senses, or a trance. However, there are many enlightened people who have had both of these kinds of experiences and they know the difference. You cannot comprehend enlightenment; it is not of the mind or body. Those who seek it sincerely find it, and those that don't seek it typically don't. Through introspection and meditation your consciousness is unbounded by the mind and a transcendent reality is realized—it's blissful. You are either in bliss or you are not. If you are in constant bliss you have entered the kingdom and don't need to be told that. You walk with Christ and live with God on earth in this eternal present moment.

• • •

Saint Paul's Christianity

Paul of Tarsus is the most enigmatic of all of Christ's disciples. He was born a Hellenized Jew in Tarsus, now a part of Turkey. He was a man of strong convictions, fortitude, and temper; just before converting to Christ, he was murdering Christians. In the beginning, Paul hated Christians. Paul is believed to be responsible for the murder of Jesus' disciple Stephen. Stephen was preaching in Jerusalem and was stoned to death (Acts 7:58). According to the Bible, Stephen became Christians' first martyr at the hands of Paul. Paul then begins to systematically go to every Christian house and arrest every Christian, men and women alike, and take them to prison, to trial, and to death (Acts 8:3, 22:4, 26:11).

We don't know how many Christians died at the hands of Paul, but we do know that Christians were so scared of him that they fled "throughout the regions of Judaea and Samaria" to avoid his wrath (Acts 8:1). The vehemence with which Paul was persecuting Christians is little known by most Christians today; the Bible tells us in Acts (9:1) that Paul was "breathing out threatenings and **slaughter against the disciples of the Lord**." The Bible says Paul (then known as Saul) "slaughters" Christ's disciples. Now Christians are running for fear of death from Paul of Tarsus. He was killing Christians for four years before he converted; he was the most anti-Christ. Now watch how the man responsible for killing the most Christians ends up taking control of Christianity. To our knowledge, Paul never even met Jesus or heard Jesus speak while he walked this earth; he didn't study with any of the twelve apostles directly before preaching, yet more than half of the New Testament is attributed to his writings.

Four years after Christ's Crucifixion, Paul was on his way to Damascus, Syria, to arrest more Christians. On his way he was struck by a light, which blinded him for some time, and "the Lord" (he believes) spoke to him from the heavens, admonishing him for his treatment of Christians (Acts 9:4 & 22:7). Seeing the error in his ways, and driven by guilt, Paul becomes a believer in Jesus and develops the idea that since he has accepted Jesus, he is now absolved of all his sin. Paul now believes God **forgives** him and Jesus has **saved** him. This new concept that Christ's sacrifice was for remission of original sin, a belief that was never adopted by the Jewish Christians who actually walked with Jesus or the Aramaic Eastern Church or the Gnostic Christians becomes the leading theme in Paul's missionary efforts to convert the Greco-Roman world to his beliefs about Jesus. This concept of sacrifice for remission of sin is another Mithran tradition practiced in Tarsus, the home of Paul, and throughout the Roman and Persian empires. The Jewish Christians called Ebionites considered Paul's teaching heresy.

How do we know that it was Christ speaking to Paul from the heavens? Moreover, if Paul had never heard Jesus speak before how did he know it was Jesus speaking? An evil force was clearly working through Paul while he was killing Christians, how do we know that that same evil inclination was not still working through him, tricking him? From what we can learn from the New Testament, Paul sure seems to have his heart into Christianity; he certainly repents, but look at how different his approach, theology, and behavior are compared to that of the twelve apostles. Paul takes it upon himself to change some of early Christians' most sacred laws and covenants, including the ones Jesus himself practiced. He essentially renounces the very religion that Christ himself observed while he lived. Paul hates the Jews so much he changes his name from the Jewish Saul to the pagan Paul and essentially reinvents himself. And we learn all this from the New Testament.

After being healed from blindness and baptized by the disciple Ananias in Damascus (Acts 9:10-17), Paul is inspired to preach. However, instead of going to Jerusalem to first learn from the masters, he goes to Arabia (Galatians 1:16) and decides to begin preaching in Damascus even though he had not ever studied the way (Galatians 1:17) . This first shot at preaching only gets him in trouble with the local Jews at the synagogue, and he is forced to flee for his own safety (Acts 9:23-25). Presumably Paul knew enough of Christ's teachings to vehemently disagree with them in Jerusalem, and he apparently did have a powerful spiritual experience in the desert. Ananias may have been instrumental in beginning to explain the way to Paul, but since Paul hasn't studied with those given personal charge by Jesus to preach we need to ask: What is he preaching? It appears that each of the twelve apostles was being stretched to understand this new teaching of Jesus, so why did Paul presume to know what to teach before being taught himself? Hearing a voice and seeing a light in the desert would be a great story to share, but how could he be preaching the way if he had not learned it yet?

Paul waited three years before going to Jerusalem again to meet with Simon Peter and James, but he wouldn't or couldn't meet with the other apostles (Galatians 1:13-24). He was not accepted by the other disciples, as they would remember him as the murderer of Stephen and other Christians (according to the church fathers). Afterward Paul left for Syria and Cilicia, where he preached and, according to Paul, they "**glorified God in me**" (Galatians 1:24). When we read the writings of the original apostles, there is a humility that they each appeared to have, but Paul is already glorifying himself. He put himself above the rest and appoints himself an apostle, apparently without discussing it with James or any of the actual twelve apostles.

Fourteen years later, after continuing missionary work in the north, Paul makes another journey to Jerusalem (Galatians 2:1-10), but he was not well received, and Barnabas went to get him and bring him back to Antioch (Acts 11:26). It is here that Paul's followers are referred to as Christians by the pagans for the first time. But Jesus' disciples didn't call themselves Christians; they were still following the way. Moreover, the first Christians from the Holy Land never accepted Paul as an apostle, or any of his scriptures; we learn this from the church fathers themselves from their letters. In fact, Professor Bart D. Ehrman, a James A Gray Professor and Chair of the Department of Religious Studies at the University of North Carolina at Chapel Hill in his course in Lost Christianities: Christian Scriptures and the Battle over Authentication states that by historical account the Ebionites, a group of Christians that actually physically walked with Jesus, never accepted Paul or this teachings. Matter of fact, they rejected him. Paul is veering away from the church in Jerusalem and the traditions of the twelve apostles and essentially establishes his own church theology that was radically different from that being practiced by Jesus' disciples in Israel.

As Paul's followings grew, so did his idea of who he thought he was for he declares himself an apostle to the Gentiles and in Galatians (1:1) Paul states that he is made an apostle "not through man, but through Jesus Christ and God the Father." So Paul becomes the self-proclaimed leader of the church to the Gentiles, making himself the thirteenth apostle (after Matthias), even though he never actually studied with Jesus or the apostles and even though most of the founding members of the church never accept him as an apostle or considered any of his writings holy scripture. Matter of fact, Paul goes on to claim almost total independence from the mother church in Jerusalem and starts preaching his own very different message. Here we see the first major division in the church, as Paul vies for control over Peter.

Even Paul's Christian traveling companions, Mark and Barnabas, leave Paul after having another dispute with him (Acts 15:36-41). Paul finally gets arrested and is nearly killed when he claimed his rights as a Roman citizen to avoid trial by the Jews. He is taken to Rome and, after writing numerous epistles in prison, Emperor Nero has him executed. But it is important to remember that Paul's writings were never accepted by the early Christians from the Holy Land; most Christians don't realize this. The church fathers tell us in their letters that Paul's writings were not accepted by the original disciples (e. g., Nazarene and Galileans), and they didn't believe Paul to be a true apostle of Christ. Paul declared himself to be one, but according to the church fathers, we know the apostles rejected him. Christians not only take on faith that Jesus is the Messiah, but also that Paul was being led by Christ in some way unfamiliar to the disciples who actually knew Christ.

Idolatry was a main concern in Judaism, and none of the original apostles would have deified Jesus because it is expressly forbidden in their religion. The first thing that Paul does with his pagan congregations to the north is make Christ an idol. Moses tells us that God said not to worship any other gods but him, Yahweh, (Exodus 20:3) and not to make idols or images (Exodus 20:4). But the Pauline sect of bishops declare him to be *homoousia*, a Greek concept which means "as the same substance" or "essence" as God. Paul places Jesus right next to Yahweh (Jehovah) in stature and importance. That's blasphemy to a Jew, and completely out of the context of the Messiah. As more pagan Gentiles began converting to Christianity, they also brought their whole pagan culture with them, and this begins to reshape the very foundation of belief in the church. Eventually the Gentile's perspective of Christ's teachings won the battle for control of the church, and their perspective is all that had been passed down to this generation, until now.

To understand the transitions made within the Jesus movement, we have only to look at what beliefs already existed in the Greco-Roman world and see what needs their civilization had to be fulfilled. Paul knew their needs and met them, and Christianity swept throughout the Roman Empire at an astonishing rate. The very roads Roman soldiers used to conquer and control foreign lands were now being used to spread Christianity. But Christianity was affected by the Greco-Roman culture as much as the Greco-Roman culture was being affected by Christianity. So next we take a look at Paul's Greco-Roman world.

Paul's Greco-Roman World

Paul is unique among Jesus' earliest evangelists in that he was not from the Holy Land (Israel-Judea); he was from Asia Minor (Turkey). His culture was pagan and, eventually, so were most his congregations. Paul's native city was Tarsus, one of the chief centers of Mithran worship. This is critical in understanding the development of Christianity in the first four centuries. **Mithra** was a god-man, born of a virgin, who performed miracles, died, and rose again and is the savior of humanity. Mithra is also the alpha and the omega, the son of God whose blood sacrifice redeems us. His followers were baptized, viewed wine as sacrificial blood, and worshiped on Sunday. The iconography is almost identical to that adopted by the Christian followers of Paul. In Payam Nabarz's book *The Mysteries of Mithras,* he describes Mithra's origins:

> **Mithra is an ancient Indo-Iranian god who was worshiped in polytheistic Persia at least as early as the second millennium BCE, and who was almost certainly related to the Vedic Mitra worshiped in India.**

Mithra was one of the most popular gods in the Roman Empire and the most favored among the Roman legions, and his iconography and philosophy were deeply engrained in the Greco-Roman world. The tradition of shaking hands with one another is believed to have originated with the Mithran cults. Mithra traces its origins to the Zoroastrian religion of Persia and to Mitra the lord of heaven in India. A hymn is dedicated to him in the Rig Veda (3.59), one of the oldest spiritual texts in the world. So, again, the transcendent god of India makes its way first to Persia and then Greece and Asia Minor, especially Tarsus, Paul's hometown where, its archetypes were adopted within Pauline Christianity.

In the Old Testament there are no precedents for or anticipation of 1) an Immaculate Conception, 2) a messianic resurrection after death, or 3) remission from original sin. These concepts are the antithesis of Judaic theology and belief; they are all pagan and especially Mithran ideologies. Jews have never believed in an immaculate conception, a virgin birth, or the divinity of their messiah. Greek gods procreate with humans, but Yahweh does not. Zeus mated with human women and had divine children, but this concept is anathema and blasphemous to Jews. Moreover, there are no "only begotten sons of God" in the Jewish religion. What the Greek version of the New Testament translates as *only begotten* (Greek *monogenes*) actually means *one of a kind* in its original Aramaic. Moreover, when Isaiah *7:14* is referenced in regards to a prophesy of a virgin birth of the Messiah, the word that is actually used is *almah*, which means a young woman (of child bearing age) and not a virgin. The Jews are expecting an heir to the throne not a divine being. Jews have never expected their messiah to be born of a virgin, but this was already an established paradigm to the followers of Mithra. The original Aramaic Bible does not include the story of the Immaculate Conception, and the original followers of Jesus believed he was the son of Joseph and Mary. Immaculate conception stories developed during the second century within the pagan cultures.

Finally, there is no original sin in Judaism; nobody needs redemption from sin, but we do need to stop sinning. The notion of original sin developed after Christ. In the original version of man's fall from grace in Genesis, as recounted in the Torah, Adam and Eve never tainted mankind, and we humans don't need to be saved from going to hell. We just need to listen to God and obey his laws, or we are going to suffer. Original sin is an adaptation. These principal tenants of Pauline Christianity are not of Jewish origin or from Christ but are all pagan ideas from within the Greco-Roman culture. Paul turns Jesus into the sacrificial lamb that is offered for atonement of sin, which is a paradigm of the Mithran cults. When Paul says (1 Cor 10:4) "They drank from that spiritual rock and that rock was Christ," he is drawing on Mithran mythology and speaking to those who understood that. Mithra was the principal messianic figure that competed with Christianity in the pagan world; eventually they were absorbed into each other and became one religion.

In *The Mysteries of Mithras: The Pagan Beliefs That Shaped the Christian World*, Payam Nabarz states that in both the Persian and Roman traditions, Mithra is seen as the savior and was born on the winter solstice (December 25th). Roman mythology shows him arising out of a rock, and the Persian mythology states that "Mithra was born of the **immaculate virgin** Mother Goddess Anahita." As Christianity was being absorbed into the Mithran cultures, it began picking up Mithran archetypes and beliefs. Quoting Nabraz again:

> **The peace-loving message of Christianity, as taught by Christ, was diminished and replaced by the warrior mindset of Mithranism.**

Death and resurrection after three days play no part in Judaism either; that is another pagan (especially Mithran) paradigm. There is no ascension story in the Aramaic version of the Bible that precedes the Greek translation. The original Jewish, Syrian, Persian, and Hindu Christians never believed in a resurrection after three days, and this story is not included in the original Aramaic Bible or the Jewish Christian Gospels. These stories were added later by the Greek-speaking followers. However, during the time of Paul of Tarsus the Egyptians, Persians, and Greeks all had numerous mythologies about **miraculous births, resurrections,** and **redemption**.

The virgin births or miraculous births are a common theme in religions around the world: Buddha, Krishna, Mithra, and Zeus all had miraculous births of divine origin. In the Hindu epic The Mahabharata, Karna was born of a virgin by the sun god Surya. The Roman god Mars and the Persian god-man Zoroaster also had divine conceptions. Death and resurrection, typically after three days, is also a common theme in the Middle East, with such god-humans as Osiris, Adonis, Tammuz, Phoenix, and Dionysus being resurrected after three days. The dominant archetype for first century civilization involved all three of these concepts, but they were completely foreign to Judaism. Judaism set itself apart from the rest of the world based on these concepts; this is what made Judaism unique in the pagan world. In fact, this is not what Jesus taught at all—this is what Paul taught.

Horus was the Egyptian sun god who was the son of god. He had a miraculous conception on December 25 from a virgin. He came to overcome darkness, and he is god's son. He heals the sick and can walk on water. After being betrayed, he is crucified, buried for three days, and resurrected. The Greek god **Attis** has a divine conception, was born December 25, is crucified, buried in a tomb for three days, and is resurrected. The Greek-Roman god **Dionysus** (Baccus) is born of a virgin on December 25. He too was crucified, buried in a tomb, and after three days is resurrected. He performs many miracles, including turning water into wine; he is god's son and he is the "the alpha and the omega."

The Persian **Mithra** was born a virgin on December 25; he performed miracles, incarnated to bring god's light into the world, and was buried and resurrected after three days. This life-death-rebirth scenario shows up in dozens of mythologies around the world, and in the first-century Middle East we have: Horus, Osiris, Amun, Baal, Phoenix, Adonis, Cronus, Cybele, Dionysus, Orpheus, Persephone, Mithras, Aeneas, Bacchus, Proserpina, Dumuzi, and Inanna who share the scenario. This metaphor was so deeply engrained in the consciousness of civilization that it grew into the Christian theology adopted in pagan lands.

Moreover, in Judaism you never make graven images of God, you don't speak of him using his sacred name, and no man is God. There were, and are, no god-men in the Bible. Even Moses, the most revered of the prophets, was still just a man that God had chosen to work his miracles through. To think that any man could be equal to God or even the son of God would be blasphemous. But Paul was competing with Cesar, a physical man who bleeds but is believed to be the descendent of the god Jupiter (Zeus) or alternatively the god Apollo who is associated with the Sun. The favorite gods of Paul's day include Zeus, Mars, and Mithra all who appear in a human form. For Jesus to compete in the pagan world, he has to assume the role of a deity and this concept becomes one of the most hotly debated subjects in the early church for the next four centuries; it's called the Arian debate.

Although scholars all agree that Jesus was not likely born on December 25, the date was chosen as it represents a powerful pagan mythology. During December 22nd to 24th the sun is at its lowest point on the horizon, and on the 25th, the sun rises again—it ascends from the darkness and is reborn. During this time the three visible stars along Orion's belt called the three kings align to the point where the sun rises again the next day. This is called the winter solstice. So we venerate the birth of the god of the sun and the Son of God on the winter solstice; we celebrate Jesus' birth on Mithra's birthday.

Father Christmas or Santa Claus is pagan, as are the Christmas tree, holly, mistletoe, and gift giving. Easter celebrates the pagan fertility goddess Eostre, Eastre, or Easter (also identified with Ishtar and Astarte), and the Easter bunny and colored eggs are a part of pagan rituals honoring the fertility goddess. Halloween is pagan, and May Day is pagan. The Sabbath that was practiced by Jesus was moved from the traditional Friday night to Saturday night to Sunday, the day the pagans worshiped the sun god Mithra. Christ's sacrifice was made during the Jewish Passover. When the Greco-Roman followers came into power, they wanted nothing ethnically Jewish in their religion, so they voted to change it to the time they celebrated the fertility goddess Eastre or Easter. By the third century, Christianity was pagan.

One of the leading theologians and apologists (advocates) for the Greco-Roman church (along with Aristides and Tatian) was **Justin Martyr** (?-100 CE). Justin wrote an influential book called *Dialogue* and helped define Pauline Christology and explain it to the pagans. He stated to them: "When we say that Jesus Christ was produced without sexual union, was crucified and died, and rose again, and ascended to heaven, we propound nothing new or different from what you believe regarding those whom you call the sons of Jupiter." None of these ideas come from the Bible; they come from paganism. The followers of Paul were putting Jesus in the same light as the Roman god-man Caesar or Mithra, as this was the paradigm of the pagan world.

The New Testament

The New Testament, also called the Greek New Testament or Greek Scriptures is the name given to the second major division of the Christian Bible, the first being the Old Testament. The New Testament gives the new covenant through the life and works of Jesus Christ. Most of it is in Koine Greek and written by various authors unknown to us. The earliest copies date from the fourth century. At present there are approximately 5,400 copies of the New Testament in Greek. Jesus spoke Aramaic, but the Gentile converts of Paul all used Greek and most of the translations we have are in Greek. As mentioned earlier, there were many changes made in the Greek New Testament that were not in the original Aramaic New Testament. According to Professor Bart D. Ehrman in his course on Lost Christianities: Christian Scriptures and the Battles over Authentication "there are more differences among our manuscripts than there are words in the New Testament." The older the version of the New Testament, the more additions and changes there are. Dr. Ehrman goes on to say that "Proto-orthodox scribes concerned about the use (or abuse) of their scriptural texts occasionally changed them to make them more useful for the orthodox cause and less available to non-orthodox Christians.", and "Even today, people sometimes base their understanding of the New Testament on passages that we do not have in the original wording."

There are twenty-seven books in the New Testament that were collected into a single volume over a period of centuries after much debate. Although some denominations differ as to which books they include in their Bible, most denominations use the same twenty-seven books that are referred to as the canon. As previously mentioned, the New Testament consists of four narratives of Jesus' ministry, called Gospels, a narrative of the apostles' ministries in the early church (Acts), twenty-one early letters (mostly Paul's) to churches and individuals called epistles, and an apocalyptic prophecy at the end called Revelation. None of the older Jewish-Christian gospels—Thomas, James, Philip, or Mary—are included in the New Testament, even though they are closer to the original source, and, thus, more historically reliable.

Moreover, none of the writings of the first Christians (Nazarenes, Ebonite's, Hebrews, etc) are included in the Greek New Testament either. Matter of fact, very little of what Jesus actually said is included; it's mostly what Paul said. Over half of the New Testament books are attributed to Paul.

The most likely candidate for authentic authorship of a New Testament book is Luke. **Luke** is believed to be the author of both the Gospel of Luke and the Acts of the Apostles. However, Luke was not listed as one of the original apostles; he's not even a Jew from the inner circle. Luke was a Syrian physician from Antioch who wrote an account of Jesus' life and possibly the book of Acts too (as it has such a similar literary and linguistic style). Moreover, Luke is repeating what he heard from others who remain unknown. In the opening lines of Acts he explains "Even as they delivered them to us, which in the beginning were eyewitnesses and ministries of the world." Luke was a follower of Paul and supported his more Greco-Roman views, so it was natural for the followers of Paul to include Luke's account of Jesus' life, for it supports Paul's pagan perspective of Jesus' message.

Mark, who is believed to be the author of the Gospel of Mark, was also not one of the original twelve apostles or an eyewitness to Jesus' ministry. He did accompany Paul and his cousin Barnabas on Paul's first missionary Journey, and possibly Peter, but he became one of Paul's closest followers (Colossians 4:10). Three gospels are called Synoptic—Matthew, Mark, and Luke—because they give a very similar narrative of Christ's life (John's Gospel is too different to be thought of as Synoptic); they comprise the core of the New Testament teaching of Jesus, and yet two of these three are not eyewitness accounts.

As Mark's is the shortest of the three Synoptic Gospels, for many years scholars believed that it was first to be written and the others, Matthew and Luke, were drawing from Mark to create their narrative; however, now many scholars think that there must have been another text that preceded these extant gospels which they call Q from the German *Quelle*, which means source. Either way, it looks like all of the Synoptic Gospels are copies of copies of copies from earlier sources not known to us. Note, Mark is still the oldest of the New Testament gospels and it does not include the immaculate conception story nor the resurrection.

During the time the New Testament was being created the entire Hellenized world was steeped in Greek mythology, especially Homer's ***The Iliad*** and ***The Odyssey***. Paul, Luke, and Paul's followers would have been very familiar with these stories. These epic stories became the basis of plays, art, and inspired literature with many spinoffs called *imitato*, and this proliferation of new versions of essentially the same story is known as *mimesis*. These New Testament accounts mimic the Greek classics. In Dennis R. MacDonald's book *Does the New Testament Imitate Homer?* he argues:

> **[T]hat the origins of passages in the book of Acts are to be found not in early Christian legends but in the epics of Homer.**

According to Dr. MacDonald, who is director of the Institute of Antiquity and Christianity at Claremont Graduate University, "early Christian authors not only fiddled with traditions and sources; they created stories after pagan literary models, sometimes without Jewish or Christian traditions to inform them." He also asserts that "Mark and Luke, I submit, borrowed from both the Jewish Bible and the Greek epics." He says ancient imitators borrowed whatever they needed from literary antecedents, including, vocabulary, grammar, names, settings, characterizations, and especially motifs, and he cites numerous examples of how the storylines in Luke, Mark and Acts have numerous parallels, sequences, composition, and prose similar to Homer's work.

In Dr. MacDonald's book *The Homeric Epics and the Gospel of Mark*, he argues that the author of Mark used the *Odyssey* as his primary literary model for chapters 1-14 and the *Iliad* for chapters 15-16, in order to depict "Jesus as superior to Odysseus and Hector, and Jesus' God as superior to the Olympians." The author of Luke-Acts also quotes Greek works, such as, Aratus's **Phaenomena** in Acts 17:28 and Euripides' **Bacchae** in Acts 26:14. There are four areas where we can see these parallels between Homer's epics and the New Testament book of Acts most clearly:

- The visions of Cornelius and Peter (Acts 10:1-11-11:18) with the dream of Agamemnon and the portent of the serpent and the sparrow in Iliad 2.
- Paul's farewell to the Ephesian elders (Acts 20:17-37) with Hector's farewell to Andromanche in Iliad 6.
- The casting of lots to replace Judas (Acts 1:15) with the casting of lots for someone to fight Hector in Iliad 7., and
- Peter's escape from Agrippa's prison (Acts 12:1-17) with Priam's escape from Achilles" bivouac in Iliad 24.

In Marianne Palmer Bonz' work *The Past as Legacy: Luke-Acts and Ancient Epics*, she argues that Luke-Acts is modeled after Vergil's Roman classic **Aeneid** (a work that also draws from Homer) stating "Luke has endeavored to interpret the underlying meaning of the whole of Christian history—and in a manner surprisingly analogous to Virgil's interpretation of the meaning of Roman history." The Aramaic-speaking Christians observed the introduction of these new Greek and Roman adaptations and rejected them, as did the Jewish followers of Christ. According to MacDonald, "Luke intended his reader to understand that he was witnessing a decisive step, perhaps the decisive step, in the expansion of Christianity into the non-Jewish world." But in so doing, the Greeks completely changed the meaning and context of Christ' word.

By scientific standards, more credence is given to those books written closest to the original source (Christ) than those gospels or scriptures written generations later. As a work passes, from one generation to the next, the chances of copying and translation errors, additions, or revisions is greater. The oldest New Testament compilation that physically is known to exist is called the Vatican Codex (Codex Vaticanus), its 759 papyrus folios date to the fourth century and are most likely from Egypt. In comparison, we have Greek manuscript sections of The

Gospel of Thomas that date back to before 200 CE—that's almost two centuries before any New Testament Gospels. Moreover, Thomas is known to have existed in Syriac or Aramaic in the second half of the first century, and the Saint Thomas Christians used a copy brought by Thomas himself in 52 CE; the fragment of the Gospel of Mary dates to approximately 60 CE.

The earliest known version of The Gospel of Mark is shorter than the modern text, too. The earliest versions of Mark don't include the last twelve verses. The last twelve verses were added later and relate to the resurrection and ascension of Jesus. The church father **Eusebius** of Caesarea wrote that he did not consider these last verses of Mark, 16:9-20, to be authentic. The ascension and resurrection stories do not appear in the older versions of the Bible, they were written in later, most likely in the second century. None of the apostles' canon had any mention of an ascension of Jesus, it's not in any of the first-century Jewish scripture, and it's not in the Aramaic Bible. In Henry Chadwick's classic book, *The Early Church,* he states:

> **Early Christians did not regard death and resurrection of Jesus to be a feature of this religion.**

He goes on to reaffirm:

> **Early Christians didn't believe Jesus died for peoples sins and rose again.**

Moreover, according to Chadwick, the way was not about "venerating Jesus for his own sake." All of these ideas were added later by the pagan followers of Paul, adopting the Mithran paradigm.

As we enter into the second century of Christian history, we see the power base move from Jerusalem to Greece and then to Rome. We see the person of Jesus develop from being a Messiah leading people to the kingdom of heaven on earth, to being "of the same substance" as

God and leading his followers in a second coming (another new concept to Jews) when the whole world (barring a few good Christians) will be destroyed. **Armageddon** is yet another pagan concept added later that was never believed by Jewish followers of Christ. The early Christians were not expecting the end of the world; they were expecting to get out of the hell they were in. The instruction went from attaining self-realization to obeying church leadership and hoping for a better next life after being redeemed for their sin from generations past.

During the next four centuries there was a power struggle for control of the church. After another Jewish rebellion against the Romans in 70 CE, the Roman Army came in force and destroyed Jerusalem, demolished the temple, and chased all the Jews and Christians out of the Holy Land. This became the death blow to the original followers of the way, and they were either killed by Romans (and later Orthodox Christians) or were effectively exiled to other lands. But the Greco-Roman form of Pauline Christianity flourished, and its story is told through the voices of the apostolic fathers, the church fathers, and the Apologists.

The Apostolic Fathers

Apostolic fathers refer to those Christian authors who lived and wrote in the second half of the first century and the first half of the second century (they precede the church fathers). They typically had either studied with or met at least one of the apostles or one of the apostles' students. Thus, they were believed to be in a succession of leadership of the church. By the beginning of the second century over fifty gospels were listed by the fathers. There was no one creed or canon at this time. Christian churches were now spread out around the Roman world, and each church used different scriptures depending on which apostle or disciple came to their city and started their church. So, what was taught varied from church to church.

The Jewish apostles taught mostly to Jews, the God fearers, and the early converts from the Holy Land and Egypt, and the areas where Aramaic was spoken, such as Syria, Jordan, and Iraq. Peter, John, Mark, and others also ventured to other lands to preach the gospel. Thomas went as far as India, but it was Paul who brought the message of Jesus (albeit his version) to the Greco-Roman world, and it was his vision of Christianity that became known to the world. Those regarded as apostolic fathers include Clement of Rome (Italy), Ignatius of Antioch (Turkey), and Polycarp of Smyrna (Turkey). They are all from Paul's lineage. As most of the church leadership in Israel and Egypt were more Gnostic in their teaching at this time, virtually all the writings of those apostolic fathers (e.g., Basilides and Valentinius) were eliminated from recognition by the new church in Rome; and many of these men were excommunicated from the church. There was an ongoing political war for control of the church, and Rome won.

Clement of Rome is considered the first apostolic father of the early Christian Church. We know very little about him personally except that he led the Church of Rome from 92-99 CE and was one of the first bishops of Rome (a pope). This Clement is not to be confused with Clement of Alexandria, a church father of the next generation who will be discussed later. Clement of Rome's first epistle to the church in Corinth is considered one of the earliest Christian documents after the New Testament and stands as an example of the political struggles that had overtaken the church. The church in Corinth is in Greece, and the congregation there had a dispute with some of their presbyters (church leaders) and removed them from office. Clement, in Rome, writes a letter to the church in Corinth and charges them with being too heavy handed and advises them to reinstate their leaders. Here we see one of the clearest examples of how the Church in Rome is taking it upon itself to dictate how a church in Greece is going to behave and who will lead it. Why wouldn't the newer church in Rome consult the more established Jewish leadership? Rome is clearly not looking for advice from the original disciples of Jesus; they are now creating their own rules and theology. The Church in Rome puts itself above the authority of the church in Jerusalem and takes over the entire movement.

In his second-century letter addressed to Theodore, Clement explains what he thinks should be done about a certain Christian group from Alexandria called the **Carpocrations**. The Carpocrations were considered Gnostic by the Church in Rome because they were followers of Mary Magdalene. The Carpocrations had a large following of women disciples and had female bishops who would give baptisms. This further supports the belief that many early Christian leaders were women, but all that changed when the Greco-Roman church began imposing its rule over the other churches. According to Clement, "A female ministry was sinful." He fears the philosophy of these apostles and considers them a threat to the status quo in Rome and wants to keep it from spreading, so he goes on to say in his second letter:

> Even if they should say something true, one who loves the truth should not, even so, agree with them...for not all true things are to be said to all men.

So the truth isn't for everyone to hear? We are not to know the truth? The bishops want to keep us from the truth, which suggests that their teachings are not the truth. So perhaps they are not teaching the truth if we are not supposed to know it. The Roman bishops don't want us to question, to think for ourselves, or know the truth; we are to listen to and obey whatever they tell us...without question. If you disagreed you could be excommunicated by the bishop, which would mean spending an eternity in hell. Now women in the ministry is a sin, bishops can send you to hell for disagreeing with them, and you are likely to get exiled, attacked, or even killed if you do. Now the Church of Rome is calling the shots. Another important factor to note is during this period, the only fathers of the church to be cited are from either modern Italy or Turkey, where Paul is from—all of those early leaders in Israel, Syria, and Mesopotamia who had differing opinions have been excluded.

Ignatius of Antioch (a.k.a. Theophorus) was the Bishop of Antioch (Turkey) who lived around 35 -117 CE. He was the third Bishop of Antioch after Saint Peter and Saint Evodius, and is an important theologian who helped develop this new line of Christian theology. Like

Clement, he was also a pagan eager to move away from the Jewish roots and was one of the first known fathers to argue in favor of changing the Sabbath from the traditional Friday night through Saturday (Jewish) to Sunday, the day for worship of the sun god Mithra. The Syrian solar religion of *Sol Invictus*, the "unconquered and unconquerable sun" (a Mithran cult), had become the all encompassing belief throughout the Roman world, and Sunday was the day this god was worshiped. So the new Church leaders, who hated the Jews and were, after all, pagan, began both worshiping on this pagan day of celebration and introducing pagan rituals into Christian worship, such as the Easter goddess and Christmas on Mithras birthday. In Ignatius' letter to the Magnesians (8:1, 9:1) he shares a view of Judaism that became universal in the Greco-Roman Church around this time (referring to the Jewish Christians):

> Be not seduced by strange doctrines nor by antiquated fables, which are profitless. For if even unto this day we live after the manner of Judaism, we avow that we have not received grace... If then those who had walked in ancient practices attained unto newness of hope, no longer observing Sabbaths but fashioning their lives after the Lord's day, on which our life also arose through Him?...It is monstrous to talk of Jesus Christ and to practice Judaism. For Christianity did not believe in Judaism, but Judaism in Christianity.

During this time the fathers of the Greco-Roman Church were establishing the importance of themselves and demarcating the bounds of their control over others. As they began consolidating their power, they began imposing a Roman-like rule over those studying the teachings of Jesus, and dissenting opinions were not to be tolerated. The bishops made themselves demigods. Ignatius goes on to say in a letter to the Smyrnaeans (8):

> Wherever the bishop appears, there let the people be; as wherever Jesus Christ is, there is the catholic Church. It is not lawful to baptize or give communion without the consent of the bishop. On the other hand, whatever has his approval is pleasing to God. Thus, whatever is done will be safe and valid.

This is one of the first times the word *catholic* (meaning universal) is used by the Church to refer to itself. Now the good Christian is no longer encouraged to find the truth for himself, or even to read or listen to scripture and learn for themselves but to listen and obey the bishop. The bishops became demigods. They then began to systematically take control of all the churches and through them, control over the minds of the faithful.

Polycarp of Smyrna (Izmir in Turkey) lived from around 69-155 CE and was believed to have been a disciple of John (presumably the apostle). His pupil was Irenaeus, who became one of the foremost church fathers. Polycarp was of great value to the church with his direct link to the apostles, which gave credence to their emerging doctrines. But not even Polycarp went along with the authority of the bishops of Rome or changing the Sabbath to Sunday, but he didn't make waves, and they agreed to disagree. He was considered less a philosopher or theologian and more of a good leader and gifted teacher.

Marcion of Sinope (Turkey, 85-160 CE) was an early Pauline Christian theologian who had a large following for some time. In his belief, Jesus was God and the man was only an appearance (docetic philosophy). He is the first Christian we know to have ever compiled a Bible—Marcion's Bible. Marcion proposed to remove everything Jewish from the Bible, the whole Old Testament, even all four of the gospels, and considered Paul the only reliable source of authentic doctrine. His canon included ten Pauline epistles and The Gospel of Marcion, which is similar to the Luke but does not include the immaculate conception story either; his conviction was that "Jesus was God," and "He" was saving us from our sin; moreover, Jesus' death on the cross was paying a "debt of sin" that all of humanity owed to God—another new pagan idea. Marcion was originally excommunicated for his views, but then years after his death, many of these views were accepted by the church. Marcion's following lasted for generations, and his ideas continue to influence Christianity even today.

Sin, Hell, and Redemption

During the second to third centuries the Greco-Romanization of Christianity introduced new concepts of what is sin, hell, and the devil, are, and why we need redemption, and it's all straight out of Greco-Roman mythology. Throughout the thousands of years of Jewish history, we have varying accounts of the afterlife and the underworld, man's sins, and salvation, but there was never the depiction of hell, as described by the Roman Christians. There are numerous references in the Old Testament to what happens to us after death, whether we have lived righteously or not, but nothing matches the descriptions of hell we start hearing in the second century, except for in Greek mythology. The devil (Hades) with his horns comes right out of Greek and Roman myths, such as, Pan (he's half goat half man) and the Satyrs.

Hades is the Greek god of the underworld, brother of Zeus and Poseidon, who together rule over the world (Zeus rules the sky and Poseidon the ocean). So the Christian devil comes from Greek mythology. The Greek underworld is also referred to as *Hades*, and the word is used in the New Testament to describe hell. When Hellenic scribes translated the Hebrew Torah into the Greek Septuagint, they used the word *Hades* to refer to hell, but the Hebrew concept of the afterlife is nothing like the Greek. There were two Hebrew concepts of hell that portray the afterlife quite differently than Roman Christians. In Hebrew **Sheol** is the "abode of the dead," the "underworld," or "pit." Sheol is the common destination of both the righteous and the unrighteous dead, as recounted in Ecclesiastes and Job.

Biblical Sheol is not a place of punishment; Hades is the gloomy afterlife of Greek mythology we think now think of as hell; so the New

Testament picks up many of those Greek archetypes. However, the two hells, Greek and biblical, are quite different. The other Hebrew reference to hell was **Gehenna**. Gehenna was a physical place on the outskirts of Jerusalem where they burned the rubbish from Jerusalem. In ancient times, it is said that children were sacrificed to the pagan god Molech in Gehenna, a practice that was later outlawed by King Josiah (*2* Kings, 23:10). The dead bodies of criminals and dead animals were left there, and fires would burn there all day and night making it look pretty grim. It was a physical place that developed into a spiritual concept but added to it was the notion of **eternal damnation**. Eternal damnation is yet another completely foreign concept to Judaism and to the original followers of Jesus, and has its origins in paganism (e.g., the myth of Sisyphus and Hades).

Eternal damnation had nothing to do with the biblical Sheol or Gehenna. We are tormented by our past sins or the estrangement from God's grace, but the afterlife is not a place of punishment. However, according to the New Testament book of Revelation (1:18, 6:8): "Hades is associated with death, and the final judgment of the wicked dead are brought out of Hades and cast into the lake of fire." According to Stephen L. Harris, chairman of the Department of Humanities and Religious Studies at California State University, Sacramento, in his book *Understanding the Bible*, Sheol is a place of "nothingness" that has roots in the Hebrew Bible and goes on to say:

> **The ancient Hebrews had no idea of an immortal soul living a full and vital life beyond death, nor of any resurrection or return from death.**

In Job (3:11-19) we learn that "All the dead go down to Sheol, and there they lie in sleep together—**whether good or evil**, rich or poor, slave or free." There is no belief in a judgment or of a reward or punishment, these are all of pagan origin, the historians and scholars are in agreement. In Professor Harris goes on to say:

> The concept of eternal punishment does not occur in the Hebrew Bible, which uses the term Sheol to designate a bleak subterranean region where the dead, good and bad alike, subsist only as impotent shadows. When Hellenistic Jewish scribes rendered the Bible into Greek, they used the word *Hades* to translate Sheol, bringing a whole new mythological association to the idea of posthumous existence.

Those who actually followed Jesus and learned under him directly and with those first twelve apostles had no notion of original sin, or the concept of punishment in hell, or eternal damnation. Moreover, Jesus did not die for our sins but rather as a martyr exemplifying complete and unconditional love and selfless service, which he was teaching. Dying for your sin was a Mithran idea that Paul propagated and was not accepted by those that walked with Christ. This pagan paradigm has been in our culture for centuries, so we assume it has always been there, but it hasn't.

In an address by **Pope John Paul II** made on July 28, 1999, His holiness explains that hell is not a place of fire and eternal suffering, but, rather, as separation from God chosen by people using their free will (http://www.vatican.va/holy_father/john_paul_ii/audiences/1999/):

"The images of hell that Sacred Scripture presents to us must be correctly interpreted. They show the **complete frustration and emptiness of life without God. Rather than a place**, **hell indicates the state** of those who freely and definitively **separate themselves from God**, the source of all life and joy."

His holiness then states that "***The* Book of Revelation also figuratively portrays in a 'pool of fire' those who exclude themselves from the book of life**, thus meeting with a "second death". So, here the leader of the largest Christian denomination, the pope, clarifies that Revelation is not to be taken literally; it is a figurative explanation for our torment when we do not know God. Hell is in our head; it's ignorance and denial of God's love and grace. Yet many preachers are still scaring and intimidating their congregations with images of a literal place where you burn, and the pope refers to these descriptions of torment as **"an improper use of biblical images."**

The early followers of the way were not anticipating a judgment day in the future or a punishment of eternal damnation in hell or some astral life in the clouds somewhere beyond Pluto (Hades), but rather the opportunity to get out of the hell they were living in under Roman oppression and into the kingdom of heaven that was at hand. In Matthew (3:2) we are advised to repent now for "for the Kingdom of Heaven is at hand" and in Matthew (10:7) Jesus tells the disciples to proclaim that "The Kingdom of Heaven is at hand." Jesus was showing us the way to the kingdom in the present moment not some time in the future. In the Gospel of Thomas when asked when the kingdom would come, Christ replies to his disciples "it will not come by waiting for it."

Pauline scriptures repeatedly try to tie the pagan, and especially Mithran, concept of dying and rising again to the Old Testament to give his beliefs legitimacy. In the Gospel of Luke (24:46) it states "Thus it is written, that the Christ should suffer and rise again from the dead the third day," and in 1 Corinthians (15:4-5) Paul states "that Christ died for our sins according to the scriptures and was buried and rose on the third day in accordance with scripture," but there is not a single reference to support this in the Old Testament. Only the Gentile followers of Paul accepted this concept because they were not Jewish and clearly didn't know the Old Testament. Paul could tell this to those who had been following Mithra but not the Jews who knew better.

In the New Testament, in the Greek translation of The Gospel of Matthew (2:23), it states that "When Joseph took his family to Nazareth he fulfilled that 'which was spoken by the prophets' He (Jesus) shall be called a Nazarene" but there is no mention of Nazareth or a Nazarene in the entire Old Testament. Matthew makes another error trying to show a fulfillment of prophesy when referring to the thirty pieces of silver Judas received for turning Jesus into the authorities (Matt 27: 9-10): "Then, was fulfilled that which was spoken through Jeremiah…"

But this reference does not appear in Jeremiah but, rather, in Zechariah (11:12-13) and is in a completely different context that has nothing to do with the fulfillment of the prophesy of a messiah or of his betrayal.

Moreover, those church leaders that did not have the benefit of gnosis themselves clearly didn't understand what those Gnostics were talking about. When you read what has been translated from the ancient codex of Gnostic literature and compare it to the church fathers descriptions of Gnostics, it becomes clear that the church fathers didn't understand the Gnostic teachings at all. Matter of fact, they completely misrepresented those teachings, just as many clergy are doing today. The Greek father's were not aware of the symbolic meanings of this Jewish-Gnostic Christianity. Nor did they have the benefit of those introspective or meditative practices of the Gnostics, so they were only seeing these teaching superficially—as pagans.

Lacking gnosis, they had to rely on old established beliefs from their pagan culture, and all the new Gentile Christian followers had to rely on what the church fathers told them. By the second century non-Jewish followers were starting to take the parables literally (which the Jews didn't). In Luke (8:10) Jesus, speaking about parables and using metaphor, is explaining how he can tell them (his inner circle) the mysteries of gnosis, but for most people he needs to use parables:

> **To you it is given to know the mysteries of the kingdom of God; but to others in parables; seeing that they might not see, and hearing they might not understand.**

So students who didn't have that higher awareness or gnosis were given parables to attempt to explain these advanced concepts. For some to have gnosis while the bishops themselves didn't was very threatening to the Greco-Roman fathers, so the Gnostics became heretics in their mind. We don't hear accounts of the church fathers feeling God bliss, but we sure do in the apostles' gospels and some of the Gnostic literature. The Pauline schools were not looking for God here and now; they were expecting to find him after death or any day when Jesus comes again. They were not experiencing those ecstatic states of higher consciousness, so the church fathers used what they did know: the pagan archetypes of their culture, and they then held onto the *hope* of a better after life or next world. Christianity met the pagan world's need for something to hope for and believe in. Christianity adapted to the culture it thrived in, which, in turn, molded it into what it is today.

So, we find no biblical precedent, from Christ himself or his original twelve apostles, dating back to the first century, that makes any claim of **redemption from original sin** from Christ's death on the cross; we find this only from Paul and from Greek revisions. Christ certainly is a redeemer; he is showing us the way to salvation through enlightenment. Redemption from original sin is not mentioned in any of the early Jewish Christian writings nor the Old Testament, the Aramaic Bible, or the apostles canon; yet in Romans (3:24; 5:9) Paul states:

> **What Christ has achieved for those who believe in him is variously described:**
> **as sinners under the law, they are 'justified by his grace as a gift'; they are 'redeemed' by Jesus who was put forward by God as expiation; they are 'reconciled' by his death; his death was a propitiatory or expiatory sacrifice or a ransom paid. The gift (grace) is to be received in faith.**

Paul just made that all up; it has no biblical precedent whatsoever. Now, according to Paul, believing in Christ alone was the only means of salvation. There was no enlightenment in this way of thinking. The theology went from achieving gnosis or a realization of one's self and God, to complete faith in what the church was representing and just believing whatever the bishops told you on blind faith. Back then very few people had a written gospel or could even read, so they depended on the bishops to interpret scripture. Within the first century the Christian movement went from God realization to faith, from heaven on earth to heaven above, and from salvation from ignorance to a physical hell and eternal damnation. You not only had to believe, you had to believe what the church told you to believe. Those that didn't listen got punished, which brings us to the next section on the church fathers. It was the church fathers who decided what we were to believe, and you won't believe what they believe.

The Church Fathers

As we move into the third and forth centuries of Christian history, we see further developments of what became the contemporary view. The church fathers are divided into two groups, those who wrote in Greek and those that wrote in Latin. This was also the time when all Hebrew and Aramaic churches, including Nazarene, Ebionite, or other non-Pauline groups were ruthlessly wiped out by the Church of Rome. None of the early church fathers from those churches who followed the way were preserved or venerated, for they challenged the authority of the Church of Rome. Those who continued to follow in the old ways were labeled heretics. By the time the church was meeting in ecumenical councils, a Jew could be burned alive for trying to keep a member of his own family from converting to Christianity.

Jerusalem had fallen and was now a Roman city, Alexandria had gone from Gnostic to Orthodox, and the churches of the Greco-Roman north began to exert more authority over those in the south. Eventually the Roman Church went so far as to completely destroy the great library in Alexandria to suppress opposing views. Books were burned, and so were people (alive). The new church viscously attacked any churches with differing views; here is where we see the final consolidation of power in Rome. To question a bishop would send you straight to hell and to question the Holy Roman Emperor would be torture and certain death.

During the third and forth centuries, Christianity had spread throughout the Roman world. In Henry Chadwick's classic book *The Early Church,* he estimates that by 250 CE there were about 100 episcopal sees in Italy alone, and by the fourth century there were **thousands of churches spread out throughout the Roman Empire.** Here we see the roles of bishops, presbyters, and deacons developed. According to historian Max I. Dimont in his book *Jews, God and History*, "At the beginning of the fourth century the Christians were the largest single religious body in the empire, though still a minority (<20 percent) of the total population." Various cities and theologians were battling, sometimes literally, for power and authority of the church. Those most prominent were called the church fathers, and they were of two camps: Greek and Latin (no Aramaic or Hebrew). The Greek fathers include Irenaeus of Lyons, Clement of Alexandria, Origen of Alexandria, and Athanasius. The Latin fathers included Tertullian, Cyprian of Carthage, Ambrose of Milan, Jerome of Stridonium, and Augustine of Hippo.

Irenaeus (?-202 CE) was Bishop of Lugdunum in Gaul (now Lyons, France). He was one of the most influential writers of Christianity, playing an important role in defining its creeds, faith, and belief. He was a disciple of Polycarp, who was believed to be a disciple of Saint John the Evangelist. He is best known for his work *Against Heresies*, where he attacks all Christian works that do not conform to the Greco-Roman or Pauline version of Christ's teachings. His focus was on the church itself, the episcopate, scripture, tradition, and authority. He was the biggest advocate of accepting episcopal authority, and the preeminence of the Church in Rome. Almost all his writings were against Gnosticism, which he includes to mean any teachings not considered orthodox by him.

In *Adverse Heresies* **he charges the Jewish Christians (Ebonite's and Nazarenes) with heresy** (volume 1, book 1, ch 26:2), first he challenges them for thinking that **"Jesus is a man and not a God"** which confirms what the historians have told us, and then pejoratively states:

> They, like Jesus as well as the Essenes and Zadakites of the centuries before, expound upon the prophetic books of the Old Testament...
> They reject the Pauline epistles and they reject the apostle Paul.

Here this leader of the church confirms that the Jewish Christians, the children and grandchildren of the original disciples who actually walked with Jesus had never accepted Paul as an apostle. They rejected Paul's Epistles and Acts and apparently never used the gospel of Luke or Revelation, and their versions of Matthew did not include the virgin birth or the ascension. The Church in Rome knew that the original followers of Jesus never accepted Paul of Tarsus. In fact, as the Nazarenes, Galileans, Syrians, Hebrew, Ebionite, and other Semitic followers rejected Paul and his theology, so the Church of Rome rejected them. Irenaeus rejected anything Jewish and referred to those who continued to observe Jewish traditions or study the earlier gospels to be **Judaizers**. He was so anti-Semite that he wanted to remove the Gospel of Matthew from the canon. He actually condemned Christians for preaching the Gospel of Matthew. He wasn't too keen on the Gospel of John either. He placed almost all the emphasis on Paul's work. By the end of the second century there were about **fifty gospels** in circulation, and by the third century there were many more, and the church fathers were trying to decide which ones to keep. Most everything was rejected. Anything Jewish, anything Gnostic had to go. Only those writing that aligned with Paul's thesis would remain.

Irenaeus knew that the families and followers of the original apostles did not believe in a virgin birth, original sin, remission of sin through Jesus, or that Jesus was a God, but he chose to deny and discount it all. He knew Jesus' followers rejected Paul's writings too and didn't consider them the true teachings of Jesus, but he chose to ignore that fact. He rejected the majority of Christian literature and aligned himself only with the beliefs that he and his sect were creating for themselves in Rome. Everything else was rejected. Irenaeus was also the first to suggest that they keep just the four Pauline gospels and remove all the other gospels, stating:

> **It is not possible that the gospels can be either more or fewer than four since there are four zones of the world, four pillars of the universe and four principal winds.**

Note, the four zones, pillars, and winds are all pagan concepts, and Irenaeus was overtly pagan. Irenaeus is also credited for explaining the role of Mary and the virgin birth and was angry that the Jewish Christians rejected their claim that she gave birth as a virgin. Here Irenaeus contrives a theology that had never existed in Judaism and was never mentioned by Jesus or his apostles: that Jesus, being born out of the Virgin Mary, created a totally new historical situation, stating:

> **Even though Eve had Adam for a husband, she was still a virgin...By disobeying, Eve became the cause of death for herself and for the whole human race. In the same way, Mary, though she had a husband, was still a virgin, and by obeying, she became the cause of salvation for herself and for the whole human race.**

Irenaeus just made that up; it doesn't exist in the Old Testament or in any of Christ's teachings. Irenaeus is also one of the major contributing theologians that 1) redefine the kingdom to mean wherever the Roman Catholic Church is, 2) clarify that the resurrection is literal and physical, and not a metaphor, 3) declare having women in the ministry is a sin, and 4) that the Antichrist was coming at the heels of Rome's eminent destruction. But more than anything else, Irenaeus was fighting Gnostics or anyone who disagreed with him. Now we have copies of the Gnostic writings that predate his by centuries, and we can see clearly that Irenaeus really didn't understand the Gnostic teachings at all, nor did he depict them accurately in his writings. He put everything but his own few books in a very disparaging light. He's right (orthodox) and everyone else is simply wrong (heretic), and those who are wrong need to be stopped. Those that disagreed with him or them were all going to hell. The threat of going to hell is what kept most people in line. The apostles themselves never excommunicated anyone, but the bishops were busy excommunicating anyone who contested them, including each other, for centuries they were sending each other to hell.

The Alexandrian School, which had previously been heavily influenced through Basilides and Valentinius, became the bridge for shifting Christian theology to orthodoxy. There were three theologians that were instrumental in shifting the Christian paradigm: Clement of Alexandria (150-211/216 CE), Origen (185-254 CE), and Athanasius (293-373 CE). Titus Flavius Clemens or **Clement of Alexandria** played a key role in reconciling the competing views of Gnostic and Orthodox Christianity. Clement *redefined* gnosis from being a personal direct experience derived from introspection, meditation, and self-inquiry to being given through **faith**. He integrates Greek Platonism into a form of Christian Platonism. He considers God to be a transcendental being and Jesus the *logos* (the Greek philosopher Plato's concept of the divine). According to Clement, both the son and the Spirit are "first-born powers and first created," this is yet another new Greek philosophy being added to Christian theology. He also advises his followers to avoid Judaiszers or those that still hold onto the ancient traditions and beliefs—the ones that Jesus and his apostles actually practiced.

Clement moved Christianity into a Greek model of good and bad, sin and evil, and made sex something dirty and impure, stating "the human ideal of continence, I mean that which is set forth by the **Greek** philosophers, teaches one to resist passion, so as not to be made subservient to it, and to train the instincts to pursue rational goals." So, here, he even tells us he is drawing upon the Greek norms and adopting them as Christian norms. They are picking and choosing what to use from the Jews and the Greeks, and in the process they are becoming increasingly more Greek and pagan.

Origen Adamantius, or Origen of Alexandria, was the disciple of Clement (of Rome) and further developed the relationship between God and Jesus and the role of the church. His book *On First Principals*, became a key reference for later Christian theologians. He too interpreted scripture allegorically and further developed the notion of Christ's divinity. For Origen, "God was the First Principal, and Christ, the Logos, was subordinate to Him." According to **Epiphanius** he wrote over 6,000 works and developed a new Christian theology that he felt could compete intellectually with Greek philosophy; he evolved Christianity into a pagan religion, with a Greek philosophical underpinning. **Athanasius** of Alexandria (293-373 CE) was a theologian who further elevated Jesus' stature to divinity, so much so that when Father Arius got up to speak at the Council of Nicea to suggest that Jesus was not "of the same substance as God," Athanasius got up and punched him in the face. Other Greek fathers of renown include **Cryril** of Alexandria, **John Chrysostom** of Constantinople, and the **Cappadocian Fathers** in modern Turkey. All deified Christ and supported the primacy of the Church in Rome.

Of the Latin Fathers, **Tertullian** (Quintus Septimius Florens Tertullianus, 160-225 CE) stands out as the most prolific and controversial, and is the first to write Christian Latin literature. He was one of the first Christian apologists (political advocate for Christianity) and polemicist against unorthodox heresy, and is sometimes known as the father of the Latin Church. Although **Theophilus of Antioch** (115-183 CE) was the first to write of "the Trinity, of God, and His Word, and His wisdom," Tertullian is credited with proposing the *trinitas* of the divine to mean "three Persons, one Substance." **Jerome of Stridonium** (347-420 CE) is best known for translating the Bible from Greek and Hebrew to Latin, which is called the Vulgate, which clearly reflects Jerome's Romanized perspective of Hebrew and Greek theology. The Vulgate is the principal biblical source for modern English translations. Jerome provides us a window to Christianity through the eyes of the Greek and Roman orthodoxy. He was also a passionate defender of the doctrine of the perpetual virginity of Mary and the superiority of being single and celibate over being married. During this time the belief that women were sinful creatures and men should stay away from them if they wanted to be pure and holy.

Augustine of Hippo or Saint Augustine (354-430 CE) is one of the most important figures in the development of Western Christianity. He was heavily influenced by Greek Platonism and is instrumental in framing the concepts of original sin and just war that became emphasized in the new Christianity. He envisioned the Church itself to be the spiritual city of God, and he initiated the medieval worldview that would later be established by **Pope Gregory the Great** (540-604 CE). He was a great advocate of papal supremacy. Much of his writing is against the Gnostic and other nonorthodox interpretations of the scriptures and the consolidation of ideologies so that the Church speaks with one voice and one authority. Quoting Richard E. Rubenstein in his book *When Jesus Became a God: The Struggle to Define Christianity during the Last Days of Rome*:

> **While Arians tended to emphasize people's potential to follow the moral example of Jesus, anti-Arians like St. Augustine focused on their continued self-enslavement, which implied the need for a Christ who was God. Only God could liberate His people from the crushing forces of habit and concupiscence.**

Other proponents of the orthodoxy include **Cyprian of Carthage** (-258) and **Ambrose of Milan** (338-397) who both advocated the Pauline perspective and denounced any Judaizing of the gospels. The focus on these fathers was now on **sin and redemption**, and purifying oneself from the passions of the mind and body. Often these men would inflict pain on themselves as a penance that they felt was spiritually purifying (mortification of the flesh); some of these practices would seem like a form of mental illness today, for example, self-mutilation, beating or whipping oneself, or wearing a hair shirt, as well as sexual abstinence. None of these were part of Christ's teachings and none of the apostles used these methods; this violent approach to ones purification is Roman.

As Christianity moves into the fourth century, its popularity spreads among the downtrodden masses of the Greco-Roman empire. It offers hope for a better life, and Christian martyrdom becomes the slap in the face to the Roman Empire that the masses rally behind. Christianity becomes a revolutionary movement within the empire. One emperor after another tries in vain to keep the movement from spreading, but those efforts to repress Christianity actually spur it on.

Within the Church we see a number of battles of theology taking place, as the Church leaders begin expanding their own roles and authority. In Rome the presbyter **Novatian** advocates the view that the Church had no power to grant remission of sin to those guilty of murder, adultery, or apostasy, but the Presbyter **Cornelius** held that the bishop could remit even a grave sin, and he was subsequently elected Bishop of Rome. Now bishops have the power to absolve sin. Ignatius insisted in the unity of the bishops and ultimate authority should be given to them stating "We ought to regard the bishop as the Lord himself." Of course, this thinking would have been completely blasphemous to any early follower of Jesus or a Jew. Moreover, **Justin Martyr** (100-165 CE) and other apologists from the Greco-Roman churches were advancing the idea that Jesus was more than a man, prophet, or messiah, but, rather, that he was God himself. This debate became known as Arianism, and it has lasted throughout the entire history of the Church.

Arianism is the theological teachings ascribed to Arius (250-336 CE), a Christian priest who lived and taught in Alexandria, Egypt. Although many sects of Christianity such as, Jewish Christians, the Syrian and Mesopotamian or Eastern Churches, and most Gnostics did not see Jesus as being the same as God or being a god, Arius was one of a large body of Orthodox Christians that held this view, and this new god-man concept was hotly debated between the churches. Arius wrote that based on Scriptures such as John (14:28) where Jesus says that "the father is greater then I" that Jesus may be of the same spiritual bloodline, so to speak, but that he himself was not God or "the same as God" (*homoousia* in Greek). This concept of a god-man has no biblical precedent, and Jesus or the twelve apostles never taught it; it's pagan. This debate lasted for centuries until the Council of Nicea in 325 CE, where the Arian teachings were considered heterodox, and Arius was branded a heretic and excommunicated by the Church. Thus another Greek idea is introduced to the teachings of Jesus, reshaping it, and moving more power to the central authority of the Church in Rome.

However, the Arian debate continued over the next century, with various ecumenical councils being convened that would reverse and overturn each other. The Orthodox Church was apparently evenly split between the two camps, with the Western churches seeing Jesus as God and the Eastern churches seeing him more as an exceptional man chosen by God. With each reversal came more contention, with bishops on both sides being excommunicated and exiled, and with many clergy and congregants being beaten and even murdered in the name of Christ. The new church was in constant battle. The church needed a leader, and out of the pagan north came a new messiah, none other than the Emperor of Rome himself—Constantine.

Emperor Constantine

Flavius Valerius Aurelius Constantinus (272-337 CE), later known as **Constantine the Great**, was the Serbian born son of a powerful Roman general named Constantius. Under Emperor Diocletian, Contantius rose through the ranks of the army, becoming governor of Dalmatia. Constantine's mother, Helena, was a Greek who Constantius later left in 288 CE to marry Theodora, the step-daughter of Maximian, ruler of the western empire. Later Constantius rose to the rank of Ceaser and was dispatched to quell the rebellions in Gaul (France) and England. During this time his son, Constantine, was being educated in Emperor Diocletian's court, where he learned Latin and Greek philosophy. It may be that he was held there as an assurance that his father did not get too ambitious and threaten Diocletian. Constantine fought for Diocletian in Asia, against the barbarians along the Danube (296), the Persians in Syria (297) and again in Mesopotamia (298), and by 305, he had become tribune of the first order. Under Diocletian the Christians were persecuted more than any other Roman emperor, and Constantine was one of his leading officers, so untold thousands died under his command.

In 305 Contantius arranged to have Constantine join him in his battles against the British, and the very next year his father died. On his deathbed, Constantius claimed Constantine Augustus, as did the local Alamannic King Chrocus, and then both Gaul and Britain quickly accepted his rule and status of Augustus (since his armies were in control of their land). Of course, normally the emperor would have to confer such a title, but Constantine sent the new emperor, Galerius, a letter with a portrait of himself in the robes of an Augustus, thus claiming the title. Rather than risk a civil war with Constantine, Galerius granted Constantine the title of Caesar but not of the more illustrious and powerful title of Augustus. During a power struggle between the designated Caesar's and coemperors' families, Maximian, the retired Ceasar, offered to marry his daughter Fausta to Constantine, so the family name would help raise him to the rank of Augustus and create a family alliance. To further support Constantine's claim to the senior rank in the empire, in 310 an orator in Gaul declared that Constantine was actually part of a dynastic line that goes back to Emperor Claudius II, and that Constantine had experienced a divine vision of Apollo that recognized Constantine as being the one who would save the world—a messiah.

In his early reign, Constantine issued coinage in honor of Mars, the god of war but later replaced the image to that of **Sol Invictus**, the unconquerable sun, a Mithran cult, which was his religion. In the summer of 311, Maxentius, who was also claiming the title Ceaser, mobilizes for war against Constantine. The night before Constantine is about to do battle with Maxentius for control of the Western empire, he is given a dream that changes the world. According to Constantine's royal historian **Lactanius**, Constantine was visited in a dream and told "to mark the heavenly sign of God on the shields of his soldiers...by means of a slanted letter X with the top of its head bent round he marked Christ on their shields (Chi X traversed by Pho P)." This was not the familiar Christian cross, that symbol was not used until later in the fourth century. Early Christians did not identify with the cross or resurrection, they used iconography of the fish, shepherd or vine and other life-affirming symbols. The church historian **Eusebius** (263-339 CE) gives us another version many years later stating that while Constantine was marching at midday "he saw with his own eyes in the heavens a trophy of the cross arising from the light of the sun, carrying the message, 'Conquer By This' (or 'in this sign conquer')." This account is not mentioned by Lactanius, however, this is what Constantine told Eusebius many years later after they became friends, and he commissioned Eusebius to write an account of his life. Although outnumbered two to one, Constantine beat Maxentius at the Milvian Bridge over the river Tiber in 312 CE.

Constantine entered Rome to popular jubilation, restored the Senatorial Curia who in turn granted him the title of the Great Augustus, but he still had Licinius in the eastern realm as coemperor. In 313 Constantine married his sister to Licinius and together they ruled, as coemperors—Constantine in the west and Licinius in the east. As coemperors, they created the **Edict of Milan** (313 CE) proclaiming religious tolerance for all religions and that property taken from Christians should be returned to Christians. This, of course, did much to rally the support of the people who had been persecuted for so long. Later, Licinius violated this pact and that gave Constantine the excuse he needed to raise an army to defeat Licinius. Then he becomes Constantine the Great, ruler of the known world and Apollo's messiah.

The Council of Nicaea

After consolidating his power throughout the Roman Empire, Constantine now directs his focus on consolidating and organizing this very eclectic form of Christianity and makes it an imperial religion under his control. In 325 CE Emperor Constantine convened a council of bishops to settle matters of dispute within the church, including the Arian controversy, the Creed of the Church, the leadership of the Church, and the date for celebrating Easter. This first of the ecumenical councils occurred in Nicaea (modern Iznik), Turkey. We are told that Constantine invited all 1,800 or so bishops from around the empire and offered to pay their way, but only around 300 (250-318) actually attended. Most of the attendees were from the Greek Church. Only five of those came from the Western Church, none of the Jewish Christians or Eastern Aramaic Churches or Gnostics are recorded as being present. So the council did not represent the majority of

Christianity but only those Pauline churches that had aligned with Constantine.

During this council, which lasted a month, they decided that Jesus was not a man but "of the same substance" (*homoousia*) as God, essentially the same "essence" as God or even the same as God. In what became known as the Nicene Creed, the declarative of Jesus' divinity was established, as was the fact of his crucifixion, the physical resurrection, remission of sin, and other Pauline doctrines. Moreover, Constantine declared that "everyone who refuses to endorse the Creed will be exiled." Constantine was now head of the Church and to contest his word was to be exiled or even executed. Even worse for a Christian was that anyone who contested the authority of the Bishop of Rome, the new Imperial church, or Constantine, would be excommunicated and marked for eternal damnation in hell.

Having declared himself an apostle, Constantine then proclaimed the Lateran Palace as the new residence of the imperial bishops, and with a stroke Christianity went from representing the poor and downtrodden to becoming the center of wealth and power in the empire. Those bishops who supported Constantine received personal attention, titles, and money; those who didn't agree with him were eliminated ruthlessly. Those who opposed him risked their life.

Constantine also formally declared the Church of Rome as the home of the first bishop and center of Christian authority, and appointed his man **Silvester** to be the first Imperial bishop. However, the final decisions about Church policy were still to be taken by the emperor. The aging bishop **Miltiades** suggested that Constantine should take charge of the Church to ensure it's protection, and he did. The next step was to inform all existing priests, including the majority that did not attend Council of Nicaea, that the Church was now formally attached to the empire, which he controlled. Those who disagreed with the creed or the decree either fled, were exiled, or were killed. The Church that had been so persecuted became the persecutors of other Christians who did not accept the Creed or the Church of Rome as the authority of the Church or that Constantine was the divine leader of their Church. Libraries were destroyed, including the great library in Alexandria in 391. Any nonorthodox writing was declared illegal and destroyed, and those that preached anything other than what Rome said were either exiled, imprisoned, or killed in the name of Christ. It was a violent purge. Gnostic writing went underground—literally.

By the fourth century Rome's Caesar became the new messiah for Christianity. He believed he was chosen by God to lead the Church, and he thought of himself as an apostle. If the other bishops didn't believe that, they certainly didn't say anything openly or contest it. Matter of fact, those at the council supported his decisions and lived happily in his palace. But this new leadership of the Church changed its theology and course radically. There are no precedents for killing anyone in Christ's name, such actions are anathema to Jesus' teachings. Yet, this man who had been responsible for persecuting Christians and leading wars in Gaul, Britain, Persia, and Mesopotamia for the power and glory of Rome and to become more rich and powerful himself, became the de facto word of God in the Church. This saint had his own wife, Fausta, murdered by strangulation in scalding water. He had his own son killed. He also had his sister's son, his uncles, and many other relatives and their friends killed; Constantine was a murdering despot. He led men to kill, rape, and steal in the name of Jesus Christ. He was as evil as any Caesar of Rome, countermanded Christ's own teachings, and led the Church in a whole new direction. This period became known as the Dark Ages.

According to Edward Gibbon, in his classic book *Decline and Fall of the Roman Empire,* Christians killed more Christians (Jewish, Syrian, and Gnostic Christians) in the first hundred years after coming into power than did the Romans during the three previous centuries. That's more than all the Christians killed by Nero, Vespasian, Titus, Domitian, Hadrian, Antonius Pius, Marcus Aurelius, Septimius Severus, Declus, Valerian, Gallienus, and Diocletian combined. **Why did Christians kill Christians in the name of Christ?** This genocide also created a near extinction of the original teachings of Jesus, only a scattering of remains to this day. Now the Roman Empire controlled the minds of men, and it was hell on earth.

Gone are the days of God is Love and looking within, instead there begins a very dark time in Christian history that includes the Inquisition, the Crusades, the Pogroms, and the Reformation all of which caused the death of millions of innocent people in Christ's name. If there was ever an Antichrist it showed it head through the actions of the Church during these times. But even as evil had entered the Church, a far greater light still shines within it to the benefit of millions of people over the past two thousand years, and that spiritual light has brought us this far. It has brought you here. We have entered the age of enlightenment. You are the proof. Here you are reading about enlightenment—you are enlightening through Christ's word. Christ's word has come to you a second time, and this second coming is enlightening you.

Conclusion

What is being suggested here is not that we throw away our old traditions, faith, or belief in God or Christ, but rather that we look even deeper into both his teachings and into our own nature; we do this to realize Heaven within—to attain God realization. Our traditions have brought us good family values, laws, and codes of conduct and morality that serve our culture so that we can better live together, but we are not going to get along well as a species if we keep killing each other over differences in what we believe. Inside every human being is a living spirit, regardless of culture, religion, or belief, and this is who or what we are; what is in our head divides us, but what is in our hearts unites us. We are all spirit, regardless of our form or the culture in which we were raised. The conflict between heaven and hell, good and evil is in your head; it's a state of consciousness. The devil is whenever or wherever you deny God's presence in your life. As we begin to see the underlying spirit in each other, we enter into a spiritual domain, and we see God everywhere, in each other and in everything, all the time—we enter the kingdom of God.

I am suggesting that we learn more about Christ's message and Christianity. The Church should lead us into Christ Enlightenment. The Church should lead us to the truth and bear the light for this global enlightenment. Our ministry should be the first to attain enlightenment. First, we need to objectively question what we've been told, and that means that you should question what I am telling you. You need to look deeper and find the truth for yourself. We need to recognize what is a tradition within the Church and what is historical fact; we need to differentiate between fiction and nonfiction, and mythology and reality. The truth brings us closer to understanding God and the expression of God on earth. We should teach our children all the facts we know, and allow the truth to deepen their faith. We need to reform and revise our understanding of Christ's teaching and bring this higher awareness to the world, so that we may all come together in peace. Enlightened Christians will invoke peace on earth through their connection with the Holy Spirit. This spirit is guiding us even now; the kingdom has come. Heaven resides within those who are enlightened in Christ or *Christ Enlightened*.

Now we have come to the point in the evolution of our consciousness where we are now ready to realize our full potential and fulfill our destiny. Once you realize that there is something to be realized, your realization has begun. Having considered this, your spirit will continue to guide you to full enlightenment. It is no coincidence that you happen to be reading this book at this particular time in your life. You have been called. You are one of the first to be chosen, as is evidenced by the fact that you are reading this book. The more you connect with your self, the more self-realized you will be, and you will be happier as a result. The more you connect with this living presence of God within you, the more you will be at one with him.

Christ has come again. His word has arisen from the ceramic crypts buried within the sands of Egypt for over 2,000 years. Your revelation is the Revelation; the Rapture is receiving his grace through the enlightenment of your consciousness. Heaven and hell are in your head; the forces of good and evil are fought within your own mind. God never left: the kingdom of heaven is right here on earth, and everywhere else. According to Christ, God lies within us and around us, in everything, everywhere, all the time. Our physical body is like a cell in the body of God; we are all part of a greater system of organizing intelligence that is life itself. The universe is alive, and we are all part of an interconnected whole. We live in an ocean of love; God's love is what sustains our existence. The more open we are to receive that love, the more we will receive it. As you enlighten you enter Eden. It's here, and it's now.

Jesus does save us from the evil inclination that tempts us and the hell that's in our own heads; he guides us lovingly into the realization of God's living presence within us, and around us, everywhere, all the time. We meet him in consciousness; we enter an awareness of God's living presence on earth, which is heaven. You are part of a relatively small but rapidly growing segment of the population that is awakening to this realization. As individuals awaken, the world awakens. Together, we are creating the critical mass that is shifting consciousness throughout the world; a higher awareness is growing within humanity. You have been led to read this book because you were ready to read it. Now, please, pass it on. The same spirit that is guiding you now to read these words will continue to guide you if you listen. Why? Because it is given to you to know. In Matthew (13:11) Jesus speaks to his disciples saying:

"Because it is given to you to know the mysteries of the kingdom of heaven."

• • •

Steven S. Sadleir

Steven S. Sadleir is a Christian and the author of several popular books, including *Looking for God: A Seeker's Guide to Religious and Spiritual Groups of the World*. He is recognized as a master in two lineages from India and serves as director of the Self Awareness Institute, which has students in over 120 countries. Steven is also host of *Enlightenment Radio*, which is picked up around the globe. He also appears in Alan Swyer's documentary *Spiritual Revolution*; Steven speaks professionally, leads seminars and retreats, and connects with students all over the world through his live teleconferenced programs.

Steven also holds a master's degree in financial economics from the University of Wales, United Kingdom (Rotary scholar), a bachelor's degree in business administration from Menlo College; he worked as an economist and investment banker before devoting himself to teaching and writing full time.

To learn more about Steven, Christ Enlightenment, the Self Awareness Institute, and upcoming teleseminars or events, to receive free downloads in MP3 or PDF format, and to receive an invitation to the next free live teleconference with Steven go to:

www.ChristEnlightened.com

List of Primary References

Chapter 1: The Prophetic Age

Bible, King James Version (Thomas Nelson Publishers, 1985)

Borg, Marcus and Kornfield, Jack, *Jesus and Buddha: The Parallel Sayings* (Ulsses Press, 1999)

Campbell, Joseph, *The Hero with a Thousand Faces* (New World Library, 2008)

Campbell, Joseph, *The Power of Myth* (New York: Doubleday, 1988)

Duffy, Eamon, *Saints & Sinners: A History of the Popes* (New Haven, CT: Yale University Press, 2006)

Kaviratna, Harischandra (Tr.), *Dhammapada: Wisdom of the Buddha* (Theosophical University Press, 1980)

Moore, Marcia and Douglas, Mark, *Astrology: The Divine Science* (Arcane Publications, 1970)

Mahesh, Maharishi, *Dawn of the Age of Enlightenment* (Int'l SRM Publications 1957)

Prasada, Rama, *Patanjali's Yoga Sutras* (Oriental Book, 1982)

Rahula, Walpola, *What the Buddha Taught* (Grove Press, 1959)

Sadleir, Steven, *Looking for God* (Self Awareness Institute, 2001)

Santillanda, Giorgio and von Dechend, Hertha, *Hamlet's Mill* (David R. Godine Publisher, 1977)

Strong, James, *Strong's Exhaustive Concordance of the* Bible (Peabody, 2007)

Swyer, Alan, *Spiritual Revolution, Eastern Spirituality in the Western World* DVD (East Meets West Productions 2008)

Vethathiri, Maharishi, *Journey of Consciousness* (Macmillan, 1992)

Chapter 2: Abraham and the Ancient World

Armstrong, Karen, *A History of God* (Gramercy Books, 2004)

Castor, Alexis Q., *Between the Rivers: The History of Ancient Mesopotamia* DVD series (The Teaching Company 2006)

Dimont, Max I., *Jews, God and History* (Signet Classic, 1962)

Dowley, Tim (Ed.), *Introduction to the History of Christianity* (Fortress, 2002)

Faulkner, Raymond, Dr, *The Egyptian Book of the Dead* (Chronicle Books, LLC, 1998)

Holland, Glenn S., *Religion in the Ancient Mediterranean World* DVD (The Teaching Company, 2005)

Lamsa, George M., *The Modern New Testament from The Aramaic* (First Aramaic Bible Society, Inc, 2001)

Leeming, David, *The Oxford Companion to World Mythology* (Oxford: Oxford University Press, need date of publication)

Levine, Amy-Jill, The Old Testament DVD series (The Learning Company, 2001).

McGreal, Ian, ed., *Great Thinkers of the Western World* (Harper Collins, 2992)

Mitchell, John, *Gilgamesh* (Free Press/Simon & Schuster, Inc, 2004)

Nikhilananda, Swami, *The Upanisads* (Ramakrishna-Vivekananda Center, 1949)

Steinsaltz, Adin, *The Essential Talmud* (Weidenfeld and Nicolson, 1976)

Singh, Jaideva, *Siva Sutras* (Motilal Banarsidass, 1988)

Singhal, K.C., *The Ancient History of India: Vedic Period* (Atlantic Publishers, 2003)

Torah (Henry Holt and Company, Inc, 1996)

Wilson, H. H. (Tr.), *Rg-Veda-Samhita* (Nag Publishers, 1977)

Zaehner, R.C., ed., *Encyclopedia of the World's Religions* (Barnes & Nobel, 1997)

Chapter 3: Judaism and the Messiah

Berg, Rav, *The Zohar*, Unabridged in English (The Kabbalah Centre International, 2003)

Berg, Philip S. Dr., *The Zohar; Parashat Pinhas* (Research Centre for Kabbalah, 1987)

Betz, Hans, ed., *The Greek Magical Papyri in Translation* (Chicago, IL: University of Chicago Press, 1992)

Cameron, James, *The Exodus Decoded* DVD (The History Channel, 2006)

Charlesworth, James H., *The Old Testament Pseudepigrapha* (Doubleday, 1983)

Eisenman, Robert (Tr.), *The Dead Sea Scrolls Uncovered* (Element, 1992)

Kaplan, Aryeh, *Sefer Yetzirah* (Weiser, 1997)

Kaplan, Aryeh, *The Bahir* (Samuel Weiser, 1979)

Matt, Daniel, *The Zohar* (Stanford University Press, 2004)

Rodkinson, Michael L., *The Babylonian Talmud* (Forgotten Books, 2008)

Tacitus, *The Annals of Imperial Rome* (Barnes & Noble, 2007)

Vermes, Geza, *The Complete Dead Sea Scrolls in English. 4th ed.* (1997) **

Whiston, William (tr.), Josephus, Flavius, *Antiquities of the Jews* and *Wars of the Jews* (Kregel, 1981)

Yonge, C.D. (Tr.), *The Works of Philo* (Hendrickson, 2006)

Chapter 4: Jeshua ben Joseph The Christ

Bauer, Walter, Kraft, Robert A. and Krodel Krodel G., *Orthodoxy and Heresy in Earliest Christianity* (Sigler Press, 1996)

Chadwick, Henry, *The Early Church* (Penguin, 1993)

Ehrman, Bart D., *Lost Christianities* (Oxford University Press, 2003)

Ehrman, Bart D., *Lost Scriptures* (Oxford University Press, 2003)

Gardner, Laurence, *The Grail Enigma* (Harper Element, 2008)

Hone, William, *The Lost Books of the Bible* (Bell Publishing, 1979)

Lamsa, George M. and Errico, Rocco A., *Aramaic Light on the Gospel of Matthew* (The Noohra Foundation, Inc., 2005)

Pashka, Joseph, *The Aramaic Gospels and Acts* (Xulon Press, 2003)

Robinson, James M., ed., *The Nag Hammadi Library* (Harper Collins, 1990)

Roth, Andrew Gabriel, *Ruach Qadim: Aramaic Origins of the New Testament* (Tushiyah Press, 2005)

Chapter 5: The Apostles' Canon

Davies, Steven tr., *The Gospel of Thomas* (Skylight Paths Publishing, 2002)

Errico, Rocco A., *Amramaic Light on James Through Revelation* (The Noohra Foundation, 2006)

Iyer, Baghavan ed., *The Gospel According to Thomas* (Concord Grove Press, 1983)

King, Karen L., *The Gospel of Mary* (Polebridge Press, 2003)

Meyer, Marvin, *The Gnostic Gospels of Jesus* (San Francisco, CA: HarperSanFrancisco, 2005)

Meyer, Marvin W., *The Secret Teachings of Jesus* (Vintage Books, 1984)

Lamsa, George M., *Idioms in the Bible Explained* (HarperOne, 1985)

Pagels, Elaine, *Beyond Belief: the Secret Gospel of Thomas* (Vintage Books, 2004)

Chapter 6: Gnosticism

Ehrman, Bart D., *The Orthodox Corruption of Scripture* (Oxford University Press, 1993)

Jonas, Hans, *The Gnostic Religion* (Beacon Press, 1963)

Jones, Christopher P., Philostaratus: Apollonius of Tyana (Loeb Classic Library, 2005)

Kasser R., M. Meyer, and G. Wurst, *The Gospel of Judas* (National Geographic Society, 2006)

King, C. W., *The Gnostics and Their Remains* (Wizard Bookshelf, 1982)

Lupieri, Edmondo, *The Mandaeans: The Last Gnostics* (William B. Erdmans Pub., 2002)

Mead, G.R.S., *Valentinus the Gnostic* (Kessinger Publishing, 2000)

Pagels, Elaine, *The Gnostic Gospels* (Random House, 2004)

Rubenstein, Richard E., *When Jesus Became God* (Harcourt, 1999)

Chapter 7: Saint Paul's Christianity

Baker, G.P., *Constantine the Great and the Christian Revolution* (Cooper Square Press, 1992)

Barnard, Leslie William, tr., St. Justin Martyr, *The First and Second Apologies* (Paulist Press, 1997)

Beck, Roger, The Religion of the Mithras Cult in the Roman Empire (Oxford University Press, 2006)

Bullock, Karen O'Dell, *The Writings of Justin Martyr* (Broadman & Holman Publishers 1998)

Butler, Samuel, tr., Homer, *The Iliad & The Odyssey* (Barnes & Nobel, 1970)

Buxton, Richard, *The Complete World of Greek Mythology* (Thames & Hudson, 2004)

Christopher, Joseph P., tr., St. Augustine, *The First Catechetical Instruction* (Newman Press, 1946)

Church, John and W. J. Brodribb, trs., Tacitus, *The Annals of Imperial Rome* (Barnes & Nobel, 2007)

Clauss, Manfred, *The Roman Cult of Mithras* (Routledge, 2000)

Cook, William R., *The Catholic Church: A History* DVD Series (The Learning Company, 2005)

Dillon, John J., tr., St. Irenaeus of Lyons *Against the Heresies* (Newman Press, 1992)

Donfried, Karl P. and P. Richardson, eds., *Judaism and Christianity in First-Century Rome* (Wipf and Stock Publishers, 1998)

Dudley, Dean, *History of the First Council of Nice* (A&B Publishers Group, 2006)

Ehrman, Bart D., *After the New Testament: The Writings of the Apostolic Fathers* DVD series (The Teaching Company, 2005)

Ehrman, Bart D., *From Jesus to Constantine: A History of Early Christianity* DVD Series (The Learning Company, 2005)

Ehrman, Bart D., *Lost Christianities: Christian Scripture and the Battles Over Authentication* DVD Series (The Learning Company, 2005)

Ehrman, Bart D., *The History of the Bible: The Making of the New Testament Cannon* (The Teaching Company, 2006)

Ehrman, Bart D., *The Orthodox Corruption of Scripture* (Oxford University Press 1993)

Healy, John F. tr., Pliny the Elder, *Natural History* (Penguin Books, 2004)

Johnson, Luke Timothy, *Jesus and the Gospels* DVD Series (The Teaching Company, 2005)

Kelly, J.N.D., *Jerome: His Life writings and Controversies* (Hendrickson Publishers, 1998)

Kleist, James A., tr., *The Epistles of St. Clement of Rome and St. Ignatius of Antioch* (Paulist Press, 1946)

Kleist, James A., tr., *The Didache* (Newman Press, 1948)

Lampe, Peter, *From Paul to Valentinus:, Christians at Rome in the First Two Centuries* (Fortress Presss, 2003)

Lenski, Noel, ed., *The Cambridge Companion to the Age of Constantine* (Cambridge: Cambridge University Press, 2006)

LeSaint, William P., tr., Tertullian, *Treatises on Penance* (Newman Press, 1959)

MacDonald, Dennis R., *Does the New Testament Imitate Homer?* (New Haven, CT: Yale Univ. Press, 2003)

Maier, Paul L., tr., Eusebius, *The Church History* (Kregel, 2007)

Nabarz, Payam, *The Mysteries of Mithras* (Inner Traditions, 2005)

Roberts, Donaldson & Cleveland, *The Ante-Nicene Fathers*, vol. III (Cosimo Classics, 2007)

Shepherd, David R., ed., *The Writings of Justin Martyr* (Shepherd Notes, 1973)

Smith, Joseph P., tr., St. Irenaeus, *Proof of the Apostolic Preching* (Paulist Press, 1952)

Ulansey, David, The Origins of the Mithraic Mysteries (Oxford University Press, 1989)

Williamson, G. A., tr., Eusebius, *The History of the Church* (Penguin Books, 1989)

Other DVD's

Banned From the Bible I & II DVD (The History Channel, 2002)

Lost Worlds: The First Christians DVD (The History Channel, 2006)

Who Wrote the Bible DVD (A&E Home Video, 1995)

The Unknown Jesus DVD (A&E Ancient Mysteries, 1999)

The Gospel of Judas DVD (National Geographic, 2006)

Online Resources

Wikipedia online encyclopedia (http://wikipedia.org/) **

The Catholic Encyclopedia (http://www.newadvent.org/cathen/)

The Gnostic Society Library, *Dead Sea Scroll Texts* (www.gnosis.org)

Institute for Antiquity and Christianity (http://iac.cgu.edu/abouttheiac.html)

Claremont Graduate University (http://www.cgu.edu)

School of Religion at CGU (http://religion.cgu.edu)

Ancient Biblical Manuscript Center (http://www.abmc.org)

Claremont School of Theology (http://www.cst.edu)

Society of Biblical Literature (http://www.sbl-site.org/)

American Schools of Oriental Research (http://www.asor.org/)

Oriental Institute: University of Chicago (http://www.oi.uchicago.edu/)

ArchNet, Virtual Library (http://archnet.asu.edu/)

Duke Papyrus Archive (http://scriptorium.lib.duke.edu/papyrus)

Journal of Religion and Society (http://www.creighton.edu/JRS/)

Early Christianity (http://www.earlychristianity.net/)

The Gnostic Library (http://www.gnosis.org/library.html)

The Vatican (http://www.TheVatican.va)

Vedanta Spiritual Library (http://www.celxtel.org)

Christ Enlightened (http://www.ChristEnlightened.com)

Book Searching (http://www.Bookfinder.com)

• • •

Sharing the Word

If you found this book inspiring, please help spread the word.

Printed copies of this book can be obtained through your local bookstore, or at:

> www.Amazon.com
> www.ChristEnlightened.com
> www.SelfAwareness.com

The Self Awareness Institute

The Self Awareness Institute and Christ Enlightened provide numerous distance learning programs from our Web sites, including:

> The Home Study Courses - engaged media learning
> The live global teleconferenced classes with Steven
> CD Sets on religion, Jesus, and Christian meditation

Dozens of downloads (some are free)
Enlightenment Radio—Google it (www.Live365.com)
We also have Study Groups around the world.

Other books by Steven S. Sadleir

Looking for God, A Seeker's Guide to Religious and Spiritual Groups of the World
Self Realization, An Owner-User Manual for Human Beings
The Awakening, An Evolutionary Leap in Human Consciousness
The Calling, A Journey Within Your Own Being

May the whole world live in peace.

Printed in Great Britain
by Amazon